PSYCHOLOGY OF
PROSPERITY

Psychology of Prosperity

Rajkumar Guddadigi

BLISS Books

Copyright © 2024 by Rajkumar Guddadigi

All rights reserved. No part of this book may be reproduced in any manner whatsoever without written permission except in the case of brief quotations embodied in critical articles and reviews.

First Printing, 2024

Contents

Dedication		vii
Achievements of this book		ix
Book Review		xi
Acknowledgement		xiii
Preface		xv
1	How My Journey Made Me a Better Person	1
2	Every Thought has Purpose	7
3	Energy in Motion is called Emotion	14
4	The Power of Self-image and Identity	20
5	Shift the Mindset by Using Belief System	27
6	Journaling: A Hacking Tool to Enter into the Brain	36
7	Why Habits and Consistency are called Secret Ingredients	43
8	Daily Rituals to Strengthen Your Roots	54

9	How Law of Karma Helps you to Live a Better Life	100
10	Conclusions	107
11	Prosperity Gift for You	110

Dedication

This book is dedicated to my mother Sharnamma Guddadigi and my late father Amruthrao Guddadigi. He is always there for me. My kid Ankush whose pure heart brings a smile on my face everyday.

Achievements of this book

#1 Release in Healthy Living & Wellness

#2 Bestseller in Stress Management

#3 Most Gifted Book in Spiritual Self-Help on Amazon

Book Review

It's a book that combines spiritual and psychological aspects and helps reader to build the great habits. All the eight chapters unfolds the amazing insight that rare to find in any book. The author has done a wonderful job by opening this book with his own life story and then discussing his personal transformation one by one.

-Manoj Sonawane, author & founder of BLISS Books

"Psychology of Prosperity" is a transformative guide to reprogramme your mind for success. Author unpacks the psychological principles behind abundance thinking and offers practical strategies for cultivating an abundance and prosperity mindset.

-Mangesh Mohan

A must buy book for everyone. This book focuses on becoming a better version of oneself by expanding our perspectives and also help us to create all great habits of life. With the help of this insight, you will be able to build your inner world and the things of the outer world will be taken care of.

-Ria Katoch

One of the most amazing book that simplify book concept and learning by using diagrams and figures in easy and efficient way.
-Hemsingh Patle, author & founder of Magical Habits

Really inspiring thoughts by the author. He has mentioned his real life story and concept in this book and that motivates us to read it till the last page.
-Prashanth Patil

It's an incredibly empowering and insightful book. This book beautifully illustrates the connection between mindset and success in every area of life.
- Manoj Barbhail

It's good read and self help book for prosperity and abundance mindset. There is no doubt that anyone can benefit from this content because it describes the author's life journey, challenges, and tools he adopted to overcome them all.
- Mahalaxmi Balaji

It's a very meaningful book which really helped me to change my way of thinking. All selected topics are really good written and covered in such a small book.
- Shabbir Shaikh

Acknowledgement

I am grateful to my sibling Anna and Avi for their support and encouragement. Gratitude to Balaji for all the support. I am thankful to my childhood friend Dharav and Pranali for always inspiring me. I am grateful to the late Mr. Datta and Mr. Nayampally for their support and my mentors Medha Ma'am, Amol Karale, and Avinash Anand Singh for sharing their valuable learning which helped me transform into a better version of myself.

I am thankful to all the beautiful souls who have supported me since my childhood. I am thankful for my previous and current organization and the people I am working with.

Special thanks to Manoj Sonawane, Hemsingh Patle and Ananda Hajare for helping me to create this book like a masterpiece and making it avail for my readers.

My dear God, thank you for all the things that have made me who I am.

Preface

This book focuses on becoming a better version of oneself by expanding our perspectives and also helps to create all great habits of life. With the help of this insight, you will be able to build your inner world and the things of the outer world will be taken care of.

The subject of neuroplasticity, quantum physics, subconscious mind programming, and self-growth is more close to my heart. I jotted down all my life learning in this book. This book also gives you scientific approach on how thoughts and emotions impact our life. All of the tools I have mentioned in this book are ones that I have personally followed and have made huge changes in my mindset and life.

May my story inspire you and the concept of this book helps you to build your new identity and become a better version of yourself.

Love and Gratitude!
Rajkumar Guddadigi

1

How My Journey Made Me a Better Person

****

"Sometimes it's the journey that teaches you a lot about your destination."- **Drake**

Writing this book gives me immense joy. My name is Rajkumar Guddadigi, born and brought up in Mumbai. I am always grateful to my parents, though they are not highly educated. My father completed his education till class 10th and left the native place Gulbarga (a district of Karnataka state, India) now called as Kalaburagi and came to Mumbai in search of job and livelihood. My mother could not go to school but she is very practical, courageous, and action taker woman.

At that time, I was living in *Chawl* (its Marathi word,

its home of meagre income people in Mumbai) of Andheri, Mumbai, India with my siblings (my elder brother and younger sister) and my parents. My elder brother was very studious, so me and my sister followed his footstep. The school we attended was St. Catherine's School, which was near our home and the medium of instruction was Marathi. School fees were very nominal in those days compared to today.

My mother had a great influence on all of us. She used to support my dad by doing the tailoring work. As a result of moving to Mumbai, she learned languages like Hindi, Marathi, and Telugu.

I still remember during the rainy season, our *chawl* used to flood with water, and we all siblings had to remove it from the room and clean the floor frequently. This was regular activity for us in rainy days. If it rained heavily, then our family and neighbours would stay awake all night for fear of rainwater entering our homes.

Since childhood I was shy and introvert. At that time, I was only concentrating on my studies. I knew that education is the only way to change our future or life situation. Thus, it became rituals for me to get better marks in any of the subject of my study. I always stood first in my class from 5th to 10th standard. Though I was good student academically but I was lacking social skill. I had low self-esteem, and low self-image. I was facing with all the problem like "Log Kya Kahenge" (what will people say?), validation, confused, no clarity in life, no confidence, no faith. My school teacher Medha Ma'am had great influence on me and challenge myself to think out of the box (I am still connected to her and she is one of the first mentor in my life journey).

A beautiful soul Pranali, my classmate we used to compete during school examination. She is very intellectual, and was a mature person at a very young age. (She is one of my accountability partners and I still discuss with her my new learning).

My sister Avi (her nickname since childhood), although I am three years older than her, she has excellent social and emotional skills and is one of my critics. I always respect her views, even if we differ on it. Along with my mother, Avi has supported me a lot in my life's journey.

I passed 10th standard and took admission in science stream. The medium of instruction in the college was English. Being a student of Marathi medium, this change was very difficult for me initially like others.

I met my good friend Dharav Shah there. We used to take a walk to college and had habit to discuss on various topic for example "why library is required ", "the advantage of having discipline in life", and many other topics like these so that we can share our views. Dharav introduced me to Swadhyaya family of Shri Dadaji Pandurang Shastri Athavaleji. They used to explain the one chapter from Bhagawad Gita on the weekly basis. I was in love with these sessions and meeting all the like-minded people there. After some time, I could not manage because of my studies. Dharav also supported me a lot in my studies (He is also one of mine accountability partner till today).

I was focused on my studies and passed out my 12th standard with first class and secured 80% of marks in PCM

(Physics, Chemistry, and Maths). I could not get admission in an engineering college. Even though college was having management quota (seats) but I was not financially sound to get that seat, so reluctantly I took admission in B.Sc. I was not happy with this admission. My dream was to do engineering and that too in chemical. 1-2 months passed like this, Maharashtra state decided to have additional seats in all the engineering colleges and that gave me a chance to get admission in Shivajirao Jondhale College, Dombivli. The fee was Rupees 8000 at that time. My family could not afford this fees. SUN, the trust supported me in paying of my engineering college fees.

I had never travelled by train before. Almost 6 hours I used to spend just in commuting. Above all, in college some students used to bully me because of my shy nature. This incidence and commuting made me sick, The result of this that I dropout in my 1st year. I failed first time in my life, I could not manage my failure and went into lowest level of my life. I was wearing the tag of failure at that time. The boy who stood first in his school and now he was dropout suddenly. You can imagine what I was feeling at that time. My self-esteem again went spirally down. My family has always supported me in my every failure especially my mother. I used to wake up early during the dropout year to earn some money by selling newspapers, washing cars, and studying as well.

SP Jain College and Bhavans college library where I used to go for study. On a few occasions security guard caught me as I was not student of that colleges and as an outsider I was not allowed to enter there. I avoided to go that library during the shift schedule of that particular security guard. That was fun. I was romancing with my study. Occasionally, I used to go to the home of one of my engineering college colleagues and study there.

Mr. Datta the founder of SUN, the Trust has embedded the habit of reading in me during that time. He was also an ex-personnel HR director at Pfizer India. He had great influence on me and my family. I am forever grateful to him for his act. He had habit of writing down problem whenever I was sharing it with him. It was his strategy to bring the solution for any problem by writing it down. He believed in me, he also had supported me financially and morally. He told me these two things:

1. If there is problem, I do not fix the problem. I fix thinking about the problem, then problem automatically resolves.
2. There is no poor people or rich people, there is only scarcity mindset and abundance mindset people.

Our parents and Mr. Datta had made sure that all three of us siblings get proper formal education and their efforts paid off after a few years. My elder brother studied electrical engineering, I studied chemical engineering, and my sister Avi became a Chartered Accountant. I am always grateful for them.

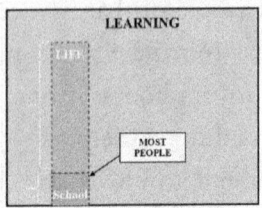

Figure 1: Life Learning

"Never let formal education get in the way of your learning"-Mark Twain

From the drop out in the first year to the final semester, all these years went peacefully. I had faith in me. Using Mr. Datta's strategy, I began to transform my failure into success. The first thing I learned was to change my thoughts and thought process. Let's learn how in next chapter.

2

Every Thought has Purpose

****

"A Man can only rise conquer and achieve by lifting up his thoughts. He can only remain weak and abject and miserable by refusing to lift up his thoughts."
- James Allen

As per oxford Dictionary: Thoughts define as an idea or opinion produced by thinking or occurring suddenly in mind. Every activity, every plan, dreams are filled with conscious and unconscious thoughts. Everything is thought. As a human we think around 60,000-70000 thoughts in a day. Out of which 95% thoughts are repetitive and majority of them are negative with no purpose. Everything in life happens twice. First in mind and second in reality. Thoughts play a very important role in shaping our life.

As a chemical engineering student and while working at site if any machine for example when boiler starts, then it generates the steam, for which we have to feed the quality fuel, likewise our mind is like a machine and thoughts gets pop up in it (or initial thoughts warm up), then it uses our body energy like fuel. They have the power to bring success or failure. Feed the quality thoughts to your mind for quality output and the energy will be used for your upliftment.

Thoughts are also like seed. Man sows a thought and reaps an action. He sows an action and reaps a habit. He sows a habit and reaps a character. He sows a character and reaps a destiny. This continues throughout our lives.

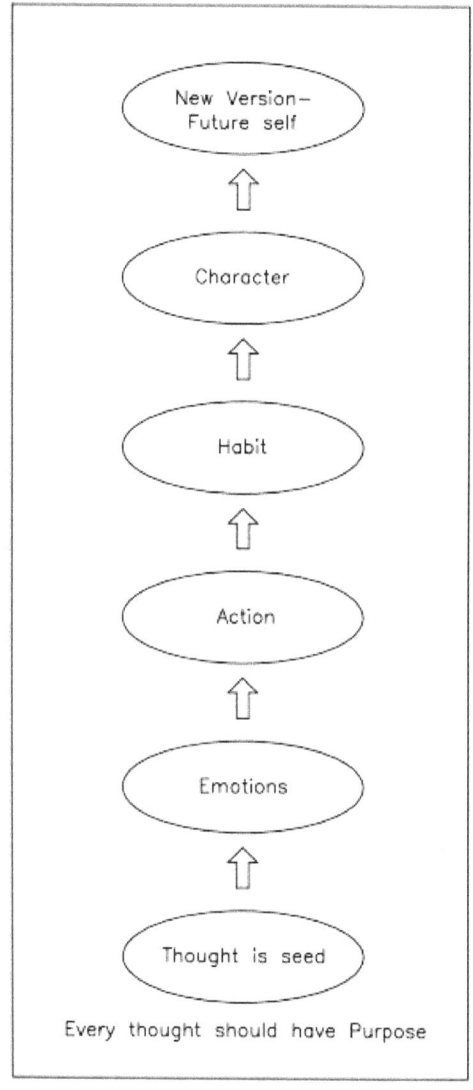

Figure 2: Every Thought has a Purpose

99% of the harm is caused in your head by your thoughts

only and among that only 1% is real harm. Most of the time, the problem is not the problem.

*The Happiness of your life depends upon the quality of your thoughts"-**Marcus Aurelius.***

Thoughts can be positive or negative. We can cultivate the positive thoughts by tendering the garden of our mind. As per neuroscience thoughts are transmitted through neurotransmitters and neurochemicals. We can proactively release positive neurotransmitter in our brain based on our thoughts only. We can change the brain chemistry by using this insight. We can heal our body and mind or make it sick by using our thoughts. The relationship between our thoughts and brain chemistry is complex and multifaceted.

According to quantum physics, our thoughts are the source of reality. Everything that we see and experience is a product of our thought energy. We are all connected through an energy field called the collective consciousness, which responds to our thoughts and emotions by creating reality.

"Protect yourself from your own thoughts" –***Rumi***

Every thought is like electric energy and that triggers the feeling. Feeling are like magnetic energy. You manifest the thing fast if you combine thought with feeling and broadcast it into your environment. For example, I have thought of buying Mercedes car (electric energy), I then decides to go to Mercedes showroom to take the test drive of this car, while driving I am feeling the comfort of the car (magnetic energy). I am generating very powerful field around me called as electromagnetic field by doing this act. This car is more likely to appear in my life if I do this. You can manifest anything by using the electromagnetic energy.

In the year 2009, children's class rice experiment was carried by Dr. Emoto. He used some plain white rice, and placed about 1/4 cup in small jars that children had brought. One jar was labelled with happy smiley face and other jar was labelled with sad and frown face. It has been told to children to think about happy, joyful thoughts in front of happy jar and sad thoughts in front of sad jar. The kids followed the instructions. At the end of one week, they brought back their jars to show the results. Upon holding the sad jar, the child had thought of cleaning his room and thunderstorms. When he held the happy jar, he had thought of a trip to Disneyland and chocolate chip cookies. The sad thought made the rice rot and change its texture (black), while the positive thought made it fresher and whiter. You can see the difference in the consistency and the mold growing in each jar (search this keyword on Google "Dr. Emoto experiment on rice". You can see the images that shows the texture of rice before and after the experiment).

Imagine what happens to our bodies inside when we have negative thoughts about ourselves? Just as a gardener cultivates his plot, keeping it free from weeds, and grows garden of flowers and fruits which he requires, so human has to tend the garden of his mind by cultivating more positive thoughts, and weeding out negatives ones. Set boundaries and distance yourself from any negativity. Trimming the dead branches is not only wise but essential for you.

The mind is a mischievous. It is like a jumping monkey.

It must be disciplined on daily basis to bring it under your control. It is only by the practical training of your mind that you can prevent bad thoughts and actions from arising and can ward off it.

Today having a positive thought is challenging considering our environment. The news, Netflix, social media we find so many content and pool of information. Thus, our mind bound to get distract and we want to consume all this information.

Instead of overloading your mind with all this information, I want you to focus on thought which gives you sense of fulfilment, and that takes you towards your goal. I have stopped watching the news and wasteful content on social media, because it lowers my energy level. My emphasis is on reading books. I read minimum 3 to 4 books in one month, listen to podcast while going to office in morning and by using it I polish my thoughts and make it great. Many great thoughts had change my perspective towards life. I have my accountability group where we discuss productive things and do mediation together. I also have friend, mentors where I sharpen my thought process further.

Here is a list of my daily rituals for disciplining my thoughts:

1. Declutter the unwanted thoughts by scribing/writing
2. Enhance the positive thoughts by reading
3. Make a peace with thought by mediation
4. Affirmation/Goal writing
5. Gratitude and Prayer

6. Physical exercise
7. Be a part of community and have an accountability partner

Let's learn how to manage your emotions in next chapter. It's crucial to regulate the emotion as it plays important factor in achieving any of your goal.

3

Energy in Motion is called Emotion

****

"Your emotions are the slaves to your thoughts, and you are the slave to your emotions."

*- **Elizabeth Gilbert***

As said by Deepak Chopra every thought, feeling, and emotion creates a molecule known as a neuropeptide. Neuropeptides travel throughout your body and hook onto receptor sites of cells and neurons. Your brain takes in the information, converts it into chemicals, and lets your whole body know if there's trouble in the world or cause for celebration. Your body is directly influenced as these molecules that course through the bloodstream, delivering the energetic effect based on your thinking and feeling.

The year 2013 was very challenging for me and my family. My Father who was detected with Pancreatic Cancer. At that time my mother stood like a rock supporting us all. I was in hospital for 3 months to take care of my father along with my family. We were all broken from the inside out by this incident. This incident of my life was like hell for me. We could not see his pain. After a lot of struggle my father rest his last breath. This was the first death I had seen in my family. Grief, sadness, frustration all negative emotions were running down in all around us. I was not knowing how to manage these feeling. Till my Journey on transformation or until year 2020, I could not understand why these type of emotions arises and how to manage it. We carry a lot baggage with us. It shatters our well-being. Slowly, I started to understand the emotions. If we say thoughts are like seed, then emotions are like fertilizer, it gives energy to our thoughts. It is now scientifically proven that emotions are like magnets. They attract the thoughts on the same wave. When we are in negative state, it triggers other negative thoughts. Based on these we create pool of negative emotions and make the situation worse.

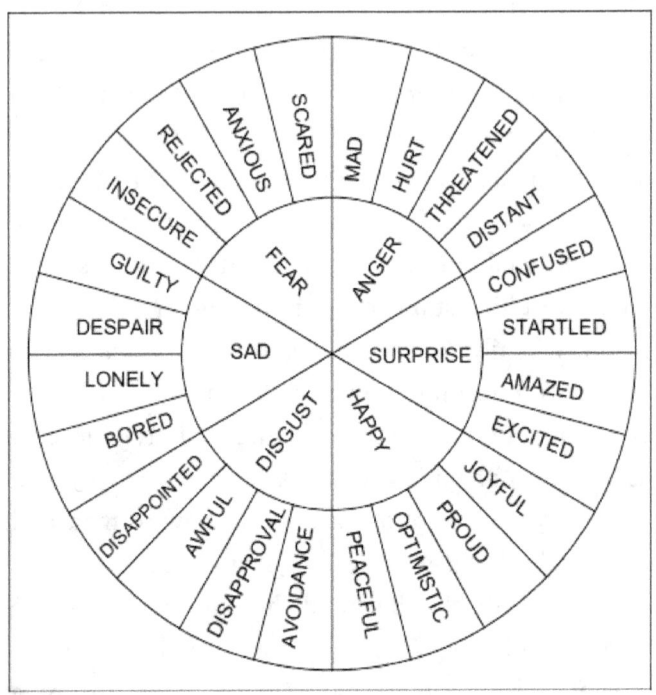

Figure 3: Different type of Emotions

Emotions are like weather. They keep changing based on our thought and our surrounding. To be happy and successful, EQ (Emotional Quotient) contributes 80 % while IQ (Intelligent Quotient) contributes 20%. The tragedy is that when I was at school, nobody taught me about EQ. (I never heard any school teaching EQ during 90s) Everyone was focusing on IQ only. EQ develops our mental health, our maturity level, that help us to understand and feel the situation and we act accordingly.

We take most of our decisions based on our emotions and feeling. During the 1970s, psychologist Paul Eckman identified six basic emotions that he suggested are universally experienced in all human cultures or race. The emotions he identified were happiness, sadness, disgust, fear, surprise, and anger. Later these emotions are expanded into more other facet as shown in Figure 3 Emotion chart.

Thoughts like "I cannot do it" "I am not enough" will automatically generate the negative emotions like sad, guilt, and despair. As per quantum physics when you feel ashamed for not being good enough you will start attracting the more thought of that belief that in turn shrinks your energy level. Be grateful for people who trigger positive emotions in you, because it is with such people that we begin to explore the possibilities of managing our emotions and life.

Elevated emotions like peace, joy, love has positive impact on our body compare to negative emotions such as shame, guilt, envy, etc. The person with elevated emotion always vibrate in a higher frequency.

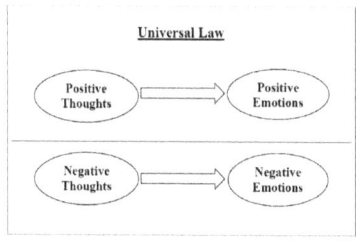

Universal Laws

Figure 4: Universal Law

Steps involved in managing the emotions:

1. Identify the emotions as per the wheel of emotions chart and feel it, express it
2. Try to write down or know the root cause of the emotions
3. Be grateful for positive things in life.
4. Change the state of your body by physiology (for example stretching your back helps you feel positive).

Let's learn more ways below:

Our Body is like pharmacy. It releases a lot of chemicals when we are exposed to any emotions. When you get trap emotionally, then best way is to move your body. Change its state immediately. There are biochemical changes in body when we move, clap or dance.

We must find ways to face and deal with the feelings that stop us from reaching our potential. By doing this we can learn the resilience.

There are numbers of advantage by simply practicing the gratitude exercise. When we are going through emotional turmoil or when we feel lost, then practice gratitude. Gratitude is the medicine which not only heal our wound but also nourishes our soul. Dissolve any emotional baggage that may be weighting you down on your life journey.

Answering the following questions can help you regulate your emotions:

1. What events or situation today caused me to feel strong? (or feeling emotionally strong)
2. How did I react to these events or situation? What were my immediate thoughts and actions?
3. Can I identify any recurring pattern in my emotional reaction or behaviour?
4. Were there any physical sensations or physical cues that accompanied these emotions?
5. Did any past memories or experience come to my mind when I experienced these emotions?
6. Are there specific people or places that tend to trigger certain emotional response in me?
7. Did I notice any changes in my mood or energy level throughout the day? what might have contributed to these changes?
8. Did I use any coping mechanisms or self-soothing techniques to manage my emotions, were they effective?
9. How did my thoughts and beliefs about myself, others or the situation influenced my emotional response?
10. What can I learn from an emotional experience today that can help me better understand and manage my emotional triggers in the future?

Your identity and self-image must be strong. More you get clarity in creating it, the more you become successful. Let's learn how to do it in the next chapter.

4

The Power of Self-image and Identity

****

"Your personality is your person reality. Your person reality is how you think, feel and act."
- Dr. Joe Dispenza

As a human we have to master following two worlds:

1. The internal world
2. The external world

The internal world consists of our thoughts, emotions, belief, habits, and stories (in the form of pattern). The inner world creates our self-image. You need to take actions to change your inner world and you can do it by recognizing its pattern. This in turn helps you to change your outer world automatically.

"The "self-image", the individual's mental and spiritual concept or "picture" of himself, was the real key to personality and behaviour. Change the self-image and you change the personality and the behaviour" - **Maxwell Maltz**

The self-image is a mental picture of how we perceive ourselves; or kind of "mental blueprint". It stores our thoughts, beliefs and emotions and is created from past experiences, failures, successes, and many other key moments of our lives.

It is basically an idea that what kind of person we perceive to ourselves. When I was kid I had idea of not speaking clearly in front of others, which I inherited as a belief and that created my self-image of not speaking with others (lacking social skills).

As a kid I went through this challenge. Initially I used to perceive that what society says about me. Nobody was there to guide me on this. Whenever I saw smart, intelligent people, I used to compare myself with them. Because of these comparisons I was building graveyard for myself as we know that each person has different background and thus the different social skills. This self-image created the disempowering belief in my subconscious mind. I started having awareness about it by reading books, attending seminar, following my mentor's advice. Slowly I started changing my image. As we know that slow and steady wins the race. Today, I take initiative to interact with people, ask them questions and connect with them.

Weak self-image is not a destiny; by right practice we can change it. We are all unique and god has gifted us one or more talents.

"The purpose of life is to discover your gift; the meaning of life is giving it away."- **Pablo Picasso.**

The low self-image damage us internally first then externally. According to Webber (2019), low self-esteem can affect everything in your life, from your relationships to your career.

Some common examples of low self-esteem:

1. Hating yourself or feeling angry or frustrated about who you are
2. Being obsessed with being perfect
3. Hating your body
4. Feeling worthless
5. Being overly sensitive
6. Feeling anxious and fearful
7. Constantly feeling angry
8. Trying to be a people pleasure

Level	Scale
Enlightenment	700+
Peace	600
Joy	540

Love	500
Reason	400
Acceptance	350
Willingness	310
Neutrality	250
Courage	200
Pride	175
Anger	150
Desire	125
Fear	100
Grief	75
Apathy	50
Guilt	30
Shame	20

Table 1: Scale of consciousness

Instead of worrying and finding the negative points in yourself, you need to keep focusing on good things of your life. Thus, you need to change your story. You need to move yourself from passenger seat to driver seat of your life. Our outer world is simply a reflection that is formed from our internal world.

If you are where you want to be right now, then you must change the internal world in order to see the change in the external world. With our thoughts, we create our world. The world is completely abundant in everything, you just need to ask the universe the right thing for you and it will be given to you in abundant way. Ask for abundant of positive thoughts.

Refer Table 1: Scale of Consciousness of this book that shows emotion like shame, guilt, apathy, grief at the lowest level (courtesy Dr. David Hawkins).

When we have low self-image, our energy level contracts and we vibrate at low frequency. In order to realize our inner self, we must be willing to live without being dependent upon opinion of others. In the book "Six Pillars of Self-esteem author Nathaniel Branden has emphasized on practice of living consciously, practice of self-acceptance, practice of self-responsibility, practice of self-assertiveness, practice of living purposely, practice of personal integrity.

By being gentle with oneself and accepting our flaws with courage and compassion, we can heal our self-image. Always live a life consciously. Accept that we are gift of god and live a life with purpose. The self-love is primary ingredient to overcome on problem of low self-esteem or low self-image.

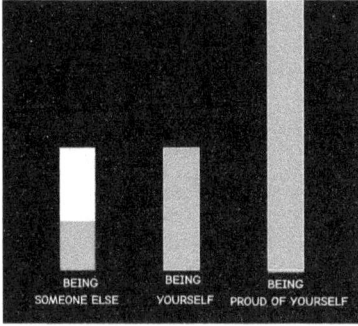

Figure 5: Self-image changes

Following are tools to create new self-image:

1. Create the new identity
2. Relax the mind and visualize new identity
3. Set the goal to achieve it
4. Empower this new belief with affirmation.

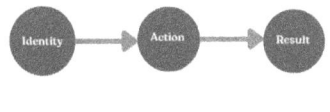

STAGES WHILE IMPROVING SELF-IMAGE

Figure 6: Stages while improving self-image

In the next chapter, let's learn about belief system. Belief is like a map without territory. The single point of difference on map causes traveler 100 of kilometers of variation on territory and have to learn how to reduce this gap.

5

Shift the Mindset by Using Belief System

****

"The outer condition of a person's life will always be found to their inner beliefs."
- James Allen

Belief plays a major role in one's life. Belief have the power to create or destroy you. What is mean by belief system. It is the thought and feeling of certainty. We develop our mindset based on our belief. Mindset is the way of thinking. It is collection of belief, perception, ideas, thoughts which influence our thinking, feeling and action.

Manushyo Vishwashen Mohit; Yatha Tatha Bhavati

Above is the verse from Bhagavat Gita that means: Man is made by his belief. As he believes, so he is.

We are born as blank slate, but as we grow, we get conditioned by society, school, friends, environment etc. This conditioning becomes our belief. One person says life is beautiful and another says life is messy. This conditioning sets our belief system. Thus, we live an entire life based on the programming that was done on us long before.

We form our belief every day. All the people around us builds our perception and that create our self-image. Thus, we can say that our self-image engraved in our subconscious mind that in turn forms our belief.

Let me share the example of Roger Bannister who was runner. Prior to his historic win in race, people believed that it was impossible to run a mile in 4 minutes by any humans on earth. But in 1954 Roger Bannister broke the 4-minute barrier by his conviction, daily practice, and rehearsed the emotional intensity of this life event in his mind. He broke this belief. After him, other 37 runners also broke the 4 minute/mile record (belief) in the same year.

The belief changes everything. Belief are generally rooted in our subconscious mind. The subconscious mind is the automatic mind. You perceive things as you believe them.

We form the belief by using following frame:

1. State of being=Thoughts +Feeling (Seconds/minutes)

2. Attitudes = Thought + Feeling (Minutes/Hour /Day /weeks)
3. Belief = Attitudes +Attitudes (Month/Year /Decades)
4. Perception=Belief+Belief+Belief   (Year/decade/lifetime)

Belief is the driving force. By positive emotions and empowering belief, we turn any idea or thought into action, then into great work.

Our life experience is based on what we focus on. Cultivating positivity is the key to unlocking the brighter future. By shifting our mindset and focusing on the good, we can manifest positive outcome and opportunities.

As we examine the origin of our current outlook, we realize that our perspective and expectation are shaped by various factors, including genes, age and life experiences. By understanding these influences, we can work towards shifting our mindset towards positivity.

Figure 7: Belief Cycle

Our approach is to actively look for the good in our lives and focus on opportunities and positive outcomes. These can be done through practices such as creating vision board, writing in manifestation journals, chanting the affirmation and speaking about your goals.

By cultivating the positive mindset, we can increase the likelihood of experiencing positive outcome and opportunities.

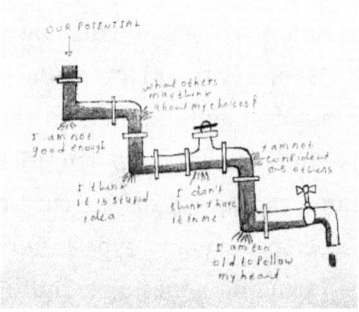

Figure 8: Energy Depletion

Do not chase the butterfly, mend your garden so that butterfly fly to it. Chasing act depletes our energy, instead you must focus on attracting the outcome. Start working on your inner self so that the outer will be taken care of.

Worrying wastes your energy. Use your energy to believe in you. Create the love, grow, glow, manifest the things and heal your life.

An individual's belief must be driven by their values. Core values refer to principles or standards of behaviour and one's judgment of what is important in life. We can achieve the deepest level of life fulfilment by deciding upon what we value most in our life, or what are our highest values. We prepare our own pain if we do not know our core value.

When I was listening one of the webinar by Dr. DeMartini about values. During that webinar, he shared his thoughts on values systems and I was inspired by them. It is given below:

"No matter how hard you try to empower your life, you'll still feel frustrated by your perceived lack of progress and achievement if you're unaware of your own values and you keep trying to live by somebody else's values".

If you do not fill your day with high priority actions that inspire you, your day will fill up with low priority distractions. If you do not bring order to your life, disorder will rule your destiny.

"Those who have a 'why'... can bear with almost any 'how'."- **Viktor Frankl,** *author of the book Men's Search for Meaning.*

I highly recommend the book Men's Search for Meaning by Viktor Frankl. My perception towards life changed after reading this book.

As written in the book Men's Search for Meaning, Viktor Frankl was kept in concentration camp, going through various pains. He explains how important it is to connect with greater meaning and purpose of life, no matter how difficult the challenges of your life are. His experience shows that even when we have no choice 'leave' or 'change' a situation, we can change how we respond to that situation.

Once you know your 'WHY', then identify the 'WHAT':

What will you need or willing to tolerate while pursuing your goal? (e.g., frustration, impatience, setbacks, failures). You can THEN plan how you might respond to each of these difficulties.

People with purpose learn and take move differently. You can see commitment in their eyes, discipline in their action and conviction in their voices. When you come across such people, you are instantly drawn to their energy. It's magnetic and that lights up your own ambitions and aspirations as well.

"Changes in perception lead to changes in outcomes".

Our positive and negative beliefs not only impact our health but also every other aspect of our life. Henry Ford was right about the power of the mind and he said this in one of his quote: "If you believe you can or if you believe you can't ... you're right."

Many limiting beliefs are formed during our childhood. Devastatingly, they become part of our identity. For example, 'I'm not good enough.' 'I am not smart, 'I do not have personality,' we think these stories are keeping us safe, protecting us from rejection and humiliation. But the fact is, they are not reality. We create meaning in our head by using these stories and that hinders our growth and we pay the cost for it.

Deep down we know we are here to shine and play big. But the stories we tell ourselves hold us back. We always play it safe. We end up living only half a life or potentials. This is where stress and internal conflict comes in. We pull ourselves from the edge of our calling.

Often, we blame external events and other people and

that put us on fear mode and we never play big. When we change our stories to create a new truth about who we really are, then we start to feel real shift.

Most of belief are so strong that they rooted in our subconscious mind. They called icebergs belief and deeply rooted and powerful and they fuel our emotions. I always wanted to write a book on my learning of abundance mindset. But I could not do it due to my limiting belief. When I listed down why this is happing. The reason behind this was that nobody has written books in my family. I decided to shift this belief.

Fear of writing was the emotions behind it. I have to empower myself and has to remove this belief by finding the purpose of writing.

My first book is now available, and there will be many more to come. If you want to achieve the things that lasts, then shift the emotions.

Famous scientist and mathematician Archimedes theorized that with a long enough lever and the right fulcrum, a man could single-handedly move the world. Your mindset is like your fulcrum while your belief is like your lever. By shifting your mindset and extending your belief of what's possible, you can magnify your ability to create what originally seemed impossible.

Belief is your compass. Your belief system is the foundation of your life. What you choose to believe will dictate how you react, think and feel. It's up to you to bring change in your life by using empowering thoughts. You need to align your beliefs with your soul's purpose to transform your life.

How add and remove the beliefs:

I am going to show you how to create a new belief system in your subconscious mind which will change your life. The power of belief resides in its ability. Let's do these four things to shift your belief:

1) Create new vision to shift the belief.

2) Then strengthen your belief with your 'will' by using affirmation.

3) Next, you become resilient with new affirmation and that further empower your belief

4) Your new belief ignites and activates itself.

Steps involve to removing limiting belief:

1. Pause, stop and reflect: If you feel fear or resistance about an activity, pause. Become aware of it.
2. Understand your thoughts are not the truth: Write down your thoughts. Try and identify the stories or 'lies' you're telling yourself. Understand that you created these 'lies' by giving meanings to events, but they are not the truth about you.
3. Look for evidence: Be aware that you have the power to turn your lies into truths by looking for evidence that is the opposite of your limiting beliefs.
4. Take back your power: Stop blaming the outside world for your results. You alone are responsible for the thoughts and actions you take in your life. Feeling anxious or stressed is, simply the result of 'low-mood

thinking'. A thought is just a thought. A feeling is just a feeling. They are not the truth about you and they will pass by like a wave of the sea.
5. Talk to someone about your limiting beliefs: It may help to express and release it. If you want to change your old (or limiting) story, then create new empowering beliefs about yourself, or to live a life of flow and inspiration, then seek out the help that you need to make this happen for you.

I use above system to add and remove belief from my subconscious mind.

Let's learn how to tap your true potentials by building the habit of journaling in the next chapter.

6

Journaling: A Hacking Tool to Enter into the Brain

****

"Once we get those muddy, maddening, confusing thoughts (nebulous worries, jitters, and preoccupations) on the page, we face our day with clearer eyes."
- ***Julia Cameron***

In the book Artist's Way Morning Pages Journal, author Julia Cameron said that journaling is, "spiritual windshield wipers." It's the most cost-effective therapy I've ever found.

"Whenever you find yourself on the side of the majority, it is time to pause and reflect."- ***Mark Twain***

As per a study by Harvard University, it was determined that journaling can be an effective tool for managing mental health, such as anxiety, depression, and stress. The Best way to reflect is to write. Write what went well, what didn't, and what you can do to make things better the next day or week. Believe me by just writing your thoughts will get the answer to most of your questions. Thus, simply grab a notebook and start journaling

Journaling about your thoughts is really simple. There's no right or wrong way to do it. You simply write down everything that comes to your mind at that time. But always start with a question. And then simply observe your mind on paper. You'll find the answer for any question you put on a piece of paper. Whenever I find difficult to think, I start writing and that makes positive impact in my life.

Every week, I put my thoughts on paper, reflect the question, and that gives more clarity to my life.

Following questions to ask to align with your vision:

1. Where did I spend most of my time this week? was it worth?
2. Did I spend most of my time that align with my long term vision why/why not?
3. How do I feel now? (rewarded /wasted time /satisfied)

Once you start putting your thoughts down on paper,

you grow exponentially in life. Here are benefits of Journaling process:

Self-awareness: We become more self-aware about our thought, feeling and experience. We start digging ourselves for self-discovery.

Emotional regulation: It can be a safe place to 'dump' what's in our heads (especially difficult feelings such as irritation, annoyance, anger). Writing makes us digest our emotions. We can learn to manage our negative emotions in a better way by doing this act.

Problem-solving: Writing create options. Option creates solution and it changes our perspective towards problem.

Creativity: We start thinking out of the box. The habit of journaling catches the idea. It stimulates our brain with imagination and creativity.

Honesty: We start accepting ourselves with flaws. Self-trust and authenticity develop. We make peace with ourselves.

Reflection: We reflect on our pattern of our behaviour, thinks based on our experience and start building tiny changes to improve our quality of life.

Gratitude: We develop the attitude of gratitude. We feel happy, joyful, abundance and appreciates the things around us.

Organized: We change our thinking patterns by writing and that helps us to organized our thoughts.

"Mediation" is one of the great book by Marcus Aurelius'

the great Roman emperor and Stoic Philosopher from 160 to 180AD. During that period, he was writing for himself in the form of journal. The book Mediation is the journal where Marcus Aurelius regulated his emotions, dealt with his fears and frustrations, so that they didn't overwhelm his life. That is why journaling is so important. Once we run through the exercise of writing daily we start regulating our emotions. Dr. Becky Kennedy therapist and child expert had said this "key to raising a happy child is to focus on emotional regulation first". Being able to name emotions and manage them effectively is the key to happiness.

By creating a habit of journaling, you can unlock new insights and perspectives that can enrich your life in countless ways. Journaling is a terrific activity to sharpen your writing skill also. Here we can record our thoughts, share our mistakes, describe our daily experience, etc. By doing this the creative juices start flowing in our life every day. By journaling, we learn how to handle our emotions and go deeper into our minds, which ultimately helps us to know ourselves better.

As per neuroscience when we start writing, many areas of brain get activated. The neurons process the information (or emotions) and creates the connections. Writing help us to be slow and think about the thoughts (or be present in the moment). When we start writing, the amygdala 'calms down' a little (tame down). Thus, getting into the habit of journaling makes our amygdala calmer and quieter. That is because we start to understand the emotions in better way, and we experience it. We also stop perceiving our imagined threats as being real. It's a key to calm down our monkey mind.

When we start writing all our sensory organs get involved. We become more focused, and build new neural connections, and that in turn make our brain more active. We think better and process and pass the information in better way. In this way, we signal to our brains to let me be present at this moment so I can focus on writing. Also, if we want to write about the past, maybe trying to heal something, and by doing it, we pass information from the long-term memory to the working memory (or short-term memory). It helps us to be faster in connecting ideas/memories/facts. When we revisit something we have already learned, we find it easier to connect, and we can build new ideas and gain new insights out of these new connections.

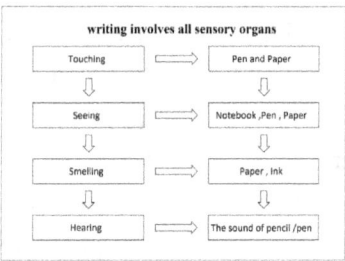

Figure 9: Senses involved in writing

"I can shake off everything if I write; my sorrows disappear; my courage is reborn". - **Anne Frank**

A simple way to begin journaling is to set an intention or to allocate 10-15 minutes each day for journaling.

Some more Journaling question to reflect and prime our self for better version:

1. What am I grateful for? This question helps us to shift our thinking in positive and happy way. Here, we show appreciation for what we have, where we are, and the love for people.
2. What is the most important task today? This question gives clarity about our priorities in any given day. Thus, we choose the most important task for the day. If you only have to do one thing today, you should do it.
3. What was the worthy moments yesterday? This question improves memory and storytelling. It can be an interesting interaction, a great conversation, or a funny moment.
4. How am I feeling right now? This question builds emotional awareness. Here we check our present feeling.
5. Lingering on problems (or emotions) that may need more attention to resolve.
6. What is working right now? What could be better way to progress in life? This question tracks goals and habit. This helps (or allow) us to correct our course of actions and keep our daily habits aligned with our goals.

Read to organize your mind. Write to record your mind. All such actions build the focus mind.

Now let's learn the importance of building great habits and consistency in the next chapter.

7

Why Habits and Consistency are called Secret Ingredients

****

"I fear not the man who has practiced 10,000 kicks once, but I fear the man who has practiced one kick 10,000 times."
- **Bruce Lee**

To understand habits, we have to understand our mind. The below picture (figure 10) shows the conscious mind is the tip of the iceberg, guiding us through the life. Our conscious mind is our thinking mind, and it's here where all the information we receive from the outside world. It determines whether the subconscious mind receives information or not. Imagine it like a filtration system, and once the conscious mind accepts the information, it makes its impression into the subconscious mind. Ideas, thoughts, imagination and creativity all are created in our conscious mind. Our conscious mind is objective mind and it has no memory, it holds one thought at a time. It gives us the sense of present moment that is feeling, doing, seeing, touching, experiencing, etc. It is easy to control the conscious mind by our choices.

The bottom of Iceberg is subconscious mind. It is silent architect of our being. Its job is to store and retrieve data. No judging, no discerning. It also ensures that we respond to the data that has been stored. In other words, if we decided at a young age that we aren't good enough in something, then that shape our life in that way, until we upgrade our programming. Our subconscious mind is subjective mind. It does not have reasoning ability; it merely obeys the commands it receives from your conscious mind. The subconscious mind can be compared to flying a plane on autopilot. It has homeostatic impulse. It keeps our body temperature at 98.6 degrees Fahrenheit, and regulates our breathing and keeps our heart beats at a certain rate.

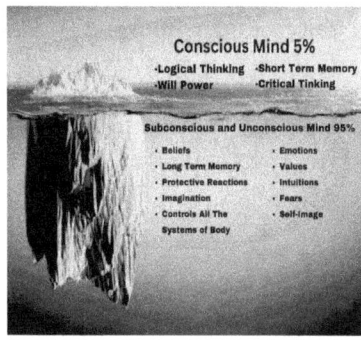

Figure 10: Conscious Mind- A Tip of Iceberg

"Your life is a printout of your subconscious program"-**Bruce Lipton**

Our subconscious mind causes us to feel emotionally and physically uncomfortable whenever we attempt to do anything new or different or to change any of our established patterns of behaviour. The sense of fear and discomfort are psychological signs that our subconscious mind has been activated. You can feel your subconscious pulling you back toward your comfort zone each time you try something new. If you think about doing something different from what you are used to, you will feel tense and uneasy. This is why breaking old destructive habits and forming new constructive ones is so challenging. Subconscious mind is the habit mind.

Learning a new skill or activity is challenging at first, but as soon as it becomes a habit or routine, it becomes easier for you to maintain. By doing so, you've reprogrammed your subconscious to work in your favour.

*"People do not decide their futures, they decide their habits and their habits decide their futures"-**F.M. Alexander***

Basically, habit is the collection of repetition /practices we do over and over. We are creatures of habit. Our daily 90% activity is governed by our habit. The way we speak, write, think, or the way we eat our food, and the road we travel to our office are already built in the form of neural pathway in our brain (habit).

Those who want to overcome the old energy draining habit and if the default conditioning of the mind is not allowing them to get rid of them (for example habits like smoking, drinking, scrolling of social media, gambling, overeating, porn, overthinking, procrastination etc.), then it indicates that they are addicted to these habits. Here, addictions are like habits only.

Sadly, we adopt the habits of other people unconsciously when we spend time with them (or the more time we spend with them, the more we become like them). We start thinking, feeling, and acting the way they do. The progress of your life depends on the type of surroundings you have. They either make your life progress easier or harder.

If you want to change this default setting, then connect with an accountability group or mastermind group (or like-minded people) that in turn helps you to create your desired setting. For example, join a book club if you want to read more, join a painting club if you want to paint more, join a fitness club if you want to exercise, or join a mediation group if you want to mediate more.

A couple of years ago, I decided to build a habit of getting up at 5 AM in the morning, so I started checking the group who get up early. I found MRM and joined this group. That was the turning point of my life. By joining this group, I learned a lot about morning rituals. I met many new people who have goals and visions in life and want to support each other in their life journey. We intentionally created a growth environment for each other and we all thrived in life. It is always easier for us to choose the right environment rather than relying solely on willpower.

The simplest way to break bad habits and create healthy ones is to join a mastermind group. It is the glue that ties commitment to your result.

In the book Atomic Habits, author James Clear has mentioned that any habits goes through the four stages (as shown in figure 11) Cue, Craving, Response and Reward. In simple terms all habits follow a pattern with starting from cue, whether its environmental or internal that creates craving. Our behavioral response follows the craving, and that results in some sort of reward.

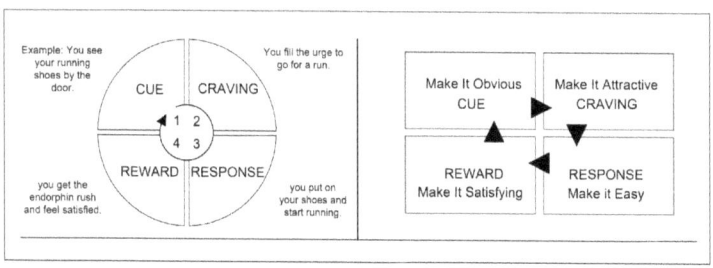

Figure 11: Habit Formation Process

The habits can be form by using following four rules:

1. **Make it obvious:** "Out of sight, out of mind". Before we take control of our habits, we need to make them visible. This means creating clear, visual cues that will trigger your habit.
2. **Make it attractive:** We have to find a way to make habit enjoyable or fun for example listening to music during workout.
3. **Make it easy:** We have to break down habit into small, manageable steps that we can easily fit into our daily routine. Do not rush in one go. Take baby steps for example starting with reading one page of book, 5 minutes of meditation, etc.
4. **Make it satisfying:** We have to find a way to reinforce the habit and make it rewarding. By tracking the habit and appreciating yourself with treat as and when you progress.

In order to create lasting change, we must first adopt a new identity and then let our habits follow it.

When everything is structured and laid out in front of you, you'll be less likely to fall into those distractions and more likely to stay on track.

To avoid depleting my energy, I follow a set routine. It includes time table like we used to do in school. Routine are best once it become habits. Those who do not have routine they feel little tense considering what next.

Routine help us to regulate our mood. It helps us to stay organized and focus on our goals. In the world of digital distraction, if we have schedule (or routine), we become more productive. We can plan the things effectively. When we have a regular routine, we are more likely to experience positive emotions such as happiness and contentment. This is because our bodies become accustomed to the routine and can anticipate what is coming next. This help us to reduce feelings of depression and anxiety, as we are less likely to be overwhelmed by unexpected events. When we have a regular routine, we are more likely to get enough sleep, exercise, and eat healthy meals and that in turn improve our physical and mental health (our overall wellbeing) or by doing it we control our environment. Routine provides a sense of stability and predictability in our lives. Another key benefit of daily routine is that they help us to streamline our cognitive energy. Many of our daily tasks are repetitive and consume valuable mental resources. However, when we have a set routine for these tasks, we can perform them more efficiently, allowing us to conserve cognitive energy for more complex and creative work. Thus, daily routines free up our creative potential. When we are consistent, the brain thrives and stress and anxiety are reduced, creating an ideal environment for generating innovative ideas.

One of the most effective ways to create a successful routine in our lives is to journal our day. We have already discussed about this in earlier chapter. Writing is the most effective way to imprint the day's activity on your mind.

Routines and habits are closely intertwined. In fact, routines often serve as a vehicle for establishing new habits.

For example, if you incorporate a daily workout into your morning routine, over time, exercising can become a habit.

Following is my routine:

Time	Routine
Morning routine	
5.30 AM to 6.30 AM	Gratitude exercise +Prayer +Mediation
6.30 AM to 7.30 AM	Visualization+Affirmation+ Incantation + Listening to Gayatri mantra
7.30 AM to 8.00 AM	Physical exercise
8.30 AM to 9.00 AM	Listening to podcasts on the way to the office
Evening routine	
9.00 PM to 9.45 PM	Journaling + Gratitude and Goal writing
9.45 PM to 10.45 PM	Mediation
10.45 PM to 11.30 PM	Reading a Book +Writing a content

Table 2: Routine Schedule

Sunday I keep for self-reflection and accountability call, and also read and write the content.

*"Growth is painful, but nothing is painful as staying in the same place "-**Mandy Hale***

Consistency compounds:

It is about the effort you bring every single day that leads to small incremental improvements. Showing up is the winning of the half battle. As persistent as those water droplets carving through rock, your unwavering dedication to your goals shapes your destiny. Stay committed to your vision, keep learning and watch as your persistent efforts yield monumental result. Consistency means doing what you have to do, even on the days when you don't feel like doing it.

GROWTH CYCLE

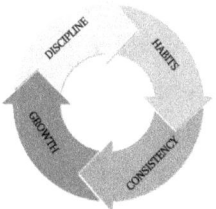

Figure 12: Growth Cycle

"The rarest of all human qualities is human consistency".
*-**Jeremy Bentham***

As Epictetus said, "When you have pain, you have the

resource of endurance." It's all inside you. You just need to dust it off and use it again.

Remember that you are stronger than you think at any given moment.

Let's take the example of growth of Chinese Bamboo tree. Although you water and fertilize the plant, you won't see any significant growth or results during the first four years.

Year 1-zero feet
Year-2 -zero feet
Year 3-zero Feet
Year 4 -zero Feet
Year 5 -90 feet in 6 weeks

The obvious question is whether the Chinese bamboo tree grew ninety feet in five weeks or five years? The answer is that it grew ninety feet in five years. If at any time during those five years if you had stopped watering and fertilizing the tree, it would have died. Many times our dreams and plans appears same like Bamboo tree. We are tempted to give up or quit trying. Instead, we need to continue to water and fertilize our dreams, or nurture the seeds of our vision.

There is saying "By perseverance the snail reached the ark" We need to be like that snail.

In 99% of cases, the reason to change comes from personal suffering, sadness, and hurt. At some point, you can't bear your current behaviour (negative emotions) anymore. Don't worry about how you will change. Focus on what habits you want to form and why. Focus on one habit in each area of your life. To me, the areas are career, health, learning, money, and relationships. For your career, you might want to show up early every day at work. For your health, you can't skip exercise regime every day. For learning, you can't stop knowing about new things in your field. As for your relationships, you cannot avoid interacting with people. For money, you cannot avoid saving for future (saving 20% of your income).

Next, we need to understand the importance of rituals to enhance the quality of our life. Let's learn it in the upcoming chapter.

8

Daily Rituals to Strengthen Your Roots

****

*"You alone are enough. You have nothing to prove to anyone." - **Maya Angelou***

If we truly want to be happier in the new era, we need to focus on developing our own virtue and character, and not linger on other people's opinions. This is possible only by performing rituals that helps you to grow in life.

*"A good character is the only guarantee of everlasting, carefree happiness."- **Seneca the Younger***

The purpose of rituals is to get you to do things that you might not want to do at the moment, but are beneficial to your long-term wellbeing. They are energy intensive. You get the much energy by doing them. The more you have it the better your life gets. The high energy people have reason for waking up early. They know their "why" when they work.

Rituals require three things: intention, attention, and repetition. By applying an intention to our habits, we force ourselves to pay attention to our bodies, thoughts, actions, and surroundings.

These are the foundation or like roots. Plants can survive the different seasons if their roots are strong, you will get fruits (or better quality fruits). We have to nourish it like Bamboo tree. Year 2020 when I was on my self-transformation journey I met my first mentor Amol Karale. I was introduced to his MRM Community and that helped me to develop the habit of getting up at 5 AM.

I started following the below rituals:

1. Prayer and Self-Love
2. Gratitude
3. Goal writing and Visualization
4. Forgiveness and Mediation
5. Affirmation and Belief incantation
6. Move your body

We will go in details step by step and discuss scientific advantage of the same. Let's take prayer first.

Prayer:

I prayed for change, so I changed my mind.

I prayed for guidance and learned to trust myself.

I prayed for happiness and realized I am not my ego.

I prayed for peace and learned to accept others unconditionally.

I prayed for abundance and realized my doubt kept it out.

I prayed for wealth and realized it is my health.

I prayed for a miracle and realized I am the miracle.

I prayed for a soul mate and realized I am the One.

I prayed for love and realized it's always knocking, but I have to allow it in.

-By Rumi

Prayer is a belief. It is communication with soul and God. When we pray we isolate us from external world, and find a peace in us.

Following story is shared by Gregg Braden about his interaction with Tibetan monk. He asked to monk "When we see your prayers on the outside – the mantras, the bells, the gongs, and the incense – what are you doing on the inside of your body? What's happening there for you?" The Monk replied "You've never seen our prayers, because a prayer cannot be seen. "What you have seen is that you created the feeling in your bodies. Feeling is the prayer". We evoke feeling by praying. Prayer is not for bargaining, negotiating or asking for some favours. Prayer changes our brain chemistry and it is like miracle. Studies has shown that different emotions activate in our body during prayer.

We feel a renewing emotion and influence our DNA to enhance wellbeing that in turn bring more coherence to the systems of our body.

Coherence can be developed by shifting our focus on our heart. It changes breath, and then emotions. But given the brain's neuroplasticity, we have the ability to change, evolve, and grow throughout our entire life span. Prayer and meditation increase activity in the frontal lobes, which are linked to attention and focus. This region also helps regulate our emotional system that reduces stress and anxiety.

Prayer stimulates serotonin (a mood stabilizer) and dopamine (the reward and pleasure system), which are chemical messengers that gets communicated to our nerves and affect how we view the world.

Studies have shown that rituals like prayer and meditation help us to reach higher level of consciousness, and more advanced levels of self-awareness that in turn literally change our brain chemistry. During prayer, there is source of energy which is bigger than us, bigger than nature working over us. Thus, God works through us by using this medium.

The Serenity Prayer:

God, grant me the serenity

to accept the things, I cannot change

the courage to change the things I can, and wisdom to know the difference.

In the morning I listen to powerful Gayatri mantra to

make me relax and bring the positive vibes around me. Reading of Hanuman Chalisa make me feel strong. After office hours I listen to Om Mani Padme Hum mantra to calm my mind and heal my body.

Self-Love:

*"You are not a drop in the ocean. You are the entire ocean in a drop"-**Rumi***

Because of my belief system my default mindset was to not love myself because loving myself meant being selfish to me. I only knew loving others like our family members, friends. The meaning behind self-love was unknown to me. When I started expanding my awareness through my mentors, books, I created the feeling of self-love. A balance between accepting yourself as you are and knowing you deserve better is self-love.

When you love to yourself, you glow from the inside. You attract people who love you, respect and appreciate you. Everything starts with how you feel about yourself. You start feeling worthy, valuable and deserve to receive the best of best things of life or it is as if you become magnetized to receive all the good things of life. The world cannot change until you change your conception about you and life.

Love is the most powerful emotions. Let's take the example of the person who is in love with someone. Because of the feeling of love his body and mind begins to change biochemically. He wants to do anything for her for the sake of love. He wants to change for her.

Self-discipline is the strongest form of self-love. Loving yourself is enough to give you everything that you ever wanted and you achieve it by self-disciplining your body and mind.

Investing in yourself is the highest ROI (return on investment) you will ever get. We often think of investment in terms of stock, real estate, hike in salary, business, etc. But what about investing in yourself. The benefit is profound. Taking care of oneself physically, mentally, emotionally, and financially is the true self love. Every moment you invest in yourself not only benefit you but also those who are around you.

Let's go more deep about self-love:

The meaning of self-love is not only loving yourself but also adopting the best of best things for your body and mind. For example, fasting has recently become more important to me since I learned how beneficial it can be to our bodies. I decided to implement it in my life. I have also stopped consuming tea or coffee with sugar and other junk food and made sure that I take care of my body like a temple. I meditate on daily basis that translates me into a focus person. Thus, it solves the goal of self-love for my body and mind.

We all are imperfect and constantly evolving to be great beings. Also you have to check whether you are competing with yourself or others as we know that competing with others we only invite anger, ego, jealousy, envy, anxiety, short term happiness, sadness, and all the other negative emotions. With self-love, you invite joy, love, hope, mindfulness, peace, gratitude, empathy, or all positive emotions of life. These elevated emotions are always good for our life and growth.

Accept as you are, celebrate your own struggle. You should be proud of how you handled life's challenges. The silent battles you have fought for your dreams will yield great results, and the time will come when you will wipe all your tears. Don't try to skip the struggle period because that is where you build your true character. The value of life is who you become in the process. Struggle is part of any success and you should accept it. My personal opinion is that things begin to change once you start to accept the struggle of your life and convert them into opportunities.

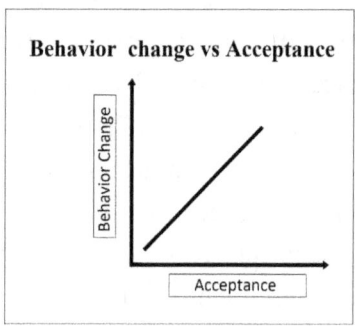

Figure 13: Behavior Change Vs Acceptance

Most people are living in an illusion and living a life of someone else's belief by comparing themselves with them. Comparison takes out all the fun of our life. But when you self-love, your uniqueness makes you awesome. You feel more than enough.

It doesn't matter where you're going in life, but every good thing you do contributes to your success. Following is also the meaning of self-love to me: surrounding myself with people who think the way I want to think. Make a conscious choice to stay with right people who see limitless possibility for their life, and who also act on their big ideas, and take positive action to make the difference in the world by adding value. Being around inspired, visionary, enthusiastic people who are living their dream is one of the fastest ways to manifest the success in your life.

I practice self-love by following rituals:

1. Prayer and being grateful in life
2. Mediation
3. Practice kindness and compassion
4. Goal writing and visualization by elevated emotions
5. Affirmation and incantations
6. Journaling
7. Physical exercise
8. New learning
9. Donation

Self-Love affirmation:
- My heart is open and I am showered with love.
- I love my hair, my body, my face, my voice. I love myself completely.

Gratitude:

"The struggle ends when gratitude begins"- **Neale Donald Walsch**

When I was kid, I was not aware of how emotions work, how to manage our emotion. when I was feeling sad, envy, anxiety, I used to hold it for many days. I still remember when I was in 6th standard, my mother complaint was that I watch too much of TV with my elder brother. My mother knew all our school teachers and principal and she told about it to them. After the prayer, our school principal called the name of mine and my elder brother. I thought she was going to appreciate about our marks, our achievement, but for my surprise she scolded us in front of all student and teachers and were mentioning that we watch a TV a lot as my mother reported it to them.

I was very upset with my mother and the school principal. The anger was there for 10-15 days. At that time, I was surrounded by negative emotions like fear and sadness. If I had known at that time the medicine called gratitude, I might not have held on to those emotions for so long.

Gratitude cannot co-exist with negative emotions. If we feel sad, jealous, overwhelm, ego, then replace these feeling with gratitude.

It is most powerful medicine which heals our emotional, mental, and physical body. It helps us to purify our soul. Tony Robbins once said "when we trade our expectations with appreciation, the entire world will change".

Cultivating a sense of gratitude for the things is the antidote to the materialistic mindset. By focusing on "what we are" attitude help us to reduce our craving for unnecessary things and that in turn helps us to find more contentment in the present moment.

When a mother gives birth to her child, qualities like compassion, resilience, confidence and passion come into her. All these are form of gratitude and that help her to connect with her new born baby.

The gratitude has become part of my life now. I started it with my "gratitude journaling". Every day I write the things I received on that particular day and that trigger my subconscious mind (that I am grateful for the things I have received today) and focus my energy on any gifts of that day (like smile given by strangers or having the ability to feed someone) and that helps me to change my perception of life. When I am going through tough situation, gratitude is the only medicine which keeps me strong because it conditions my mind for positive aspects of life.

Greatness starts with being grateful. Many things may be going wrong in your life but there are many things are going right as well. Gratitude is a contagious emotion. If you express gratitude often, people will like to help you and will work with you.

With gratitude, you can start to train your mind to appreciate what you already have, and by doing that more opportunities come your way. You will create many opportunities for business or better life. Gratitude can convert frustration and scarcity into acceptance and abundance. Start practicing daily to build your gratitude muscle.

Appreciation and gratitude help create joy and peace within us. Therefore, when we feel gratitude, we are creating more abundance and prosperity in our lives. Like energy attracts like energy. Like if you grateful for love given by someone else, then more loving people will come into your life. Studies have shown that gratitude fosters adaptive coping mechanisms. By managing positive emotions like satisfaction, happiness, pleasure, and gratitude we enhance our emotional resilience and builds our inner strength to combat any stress. When we embrace gratitude, we are sending a powerful message to the universe that we appreciate what we have. This act of acknowledging the things of life opens the door for more abundance into our life. People who seem to be more grateful are also more altruistic.

As said that thankfulness is wonder medicine, if it is considered pill then it would be world's bestselling product and that will take care of maintenance of every part of our body. **Gratitude =Happiness + Joy + Peace + Health.**

Remember this line "It is not happiness that brings us gratitude. It is gratitude that brings us happiness".

Most of the time Instant gratification hold us back and that trap us into the short term happiness. It involves addiction to porn, junk food, alcohol, Netflix, social media, etc. Convert all the instant gratification into delayed gratification like building muscle of your body or business. You'll feel worthy of doing it.

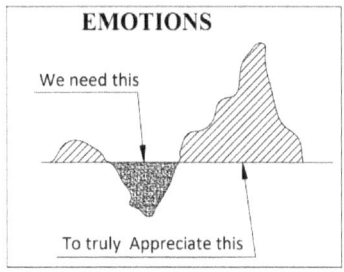

Figure 14: Gratitude of Emotions

Here is what my guru Avinash Anand Singh said about Gratitude:

"Gratitude is the way to create a great life".

"When things are not going well, be grateful".

"When there are challenges, be grateful".

"When feeling low and sad, be grateful".

"When you want to manifest, be grateful".

The more life brings adversities; the more gratitude we must offer. Gratitude is the currency of abundance and peace. If you practice it, it can shift/change your entire life. Life stands behind grateful heart (person).

Gratitude is a powerful catalyst for change and shifts the perspective of the thing you have in your hand and that in turn helps you to rewire your brain for optimism and openness. It then lays the foundation for personal transformation.

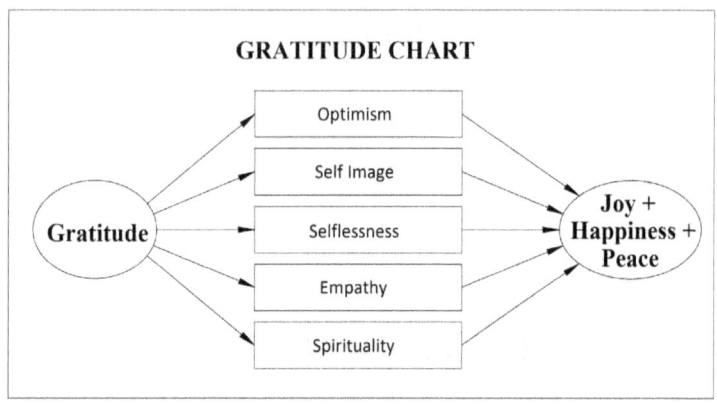

Figure 15: Gratitude of Chart

As per study following are the benefits of practicing gratitude in our daily routine:

1. Gratitude promotes higher self-esteem
2. Gratitude makes you less materialistic
3. Gratitude can help you sleep better
4. Gratitude can help you relieve stress
5. Gratitude can make you feel more positive emotions
6. Gratitude can help you calm down in tough moments
7. Gratitude strengthens your social relationships
8. Gratitude helps you understand others better
9. Gratitude helps you recognize how much you have
10. Gratitude puts you at a lower risk of depression
11. Gratitude promotes a more positive outlook of life
12. Gratitude promotes selflessness

We can cultivate the attitude of Gratitude by using following steps:

1. Keeping a gratitude journal
2. Thank someone mentally
3. Write a thank-you note
4. Bless the planet earth, people, animal kingdom and plant kingdom in your prayer and meditations

Goals and Vision:
Visions:
"If you are working on something exciting that you really care about, you don't have to be pushed. The vision pulls you."
-Steve Jobs

Imagine a painter standing in front of blank canvas. He has the creativity and potentials to create anything by dreaming, thinking big, generating colourful experiences and new ideas. Vision is the one which brings colourful ideas for our future self. It always inspires us and keep excitement in our life. Vision and goals guide our life path. The vision must align with your deepest values and priorities. It brings purpose, meaning and brightens our life. It always pushes you beyond your boundaries, and helps you to find the solution during unknown or difficult situation. It challenges you if you fall back into your comfort zone. It tests your true potential. You begin to think about why you exist (by developing vision), what gifts I am having and how can I share it with the world.

There is saying that vision is art of seeing what is

invisible to others. Vision is insight and resides deep down within us. It needs a lot of efforts to bring it up. Throughout history, progress has only been made by people who "saw" things before they actually happened. Vision is seeing the future before it comes into being.

Vision can be applied in life by using the steps shown in the figure 16.

Your vision board must emit positive energy. Also, our subconscious mind understands the language of colours and manifest it fast if we convert our vision into colourful photos. Thus, when we need to add pictures or images in our vision while preparing it. I personally have my vision board where I can see the picture of my future self in these five circles. I have put my five years goals in it.

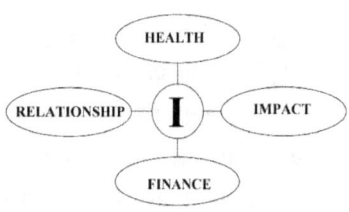

Figure 16: Areas of Five Years Vision

Thinking	Acting	Praying/ Visualization/ Feeling
1) Asking the question about our existence	1) Listing down the unique gifts, personal qualities, interest, etc.	1) Pray to god to see the vision
2) Discovering our "why", or Purpose of life	2) Refining and Polishing the gifts	2) With elevated emotions feel the visions/gifts by using the visualization and mediation tools
3) What is my dreams, inspiration	3) What action do I need to take to make this happens and how can I make it easier for myself to take these action?	3) Images will help to feel the elevated emotions and see clearly what I want to achieve
4) What does it mean for me to have a good area of life? and what do I have to do to achieve it.	4) Join the mastermind group	4) Affirmation, words, incantation help us to keep going on low days

5) How will I feel if I have good area of life and how can I feel those feeling right now.	5) Find the Gurus to accomplish your dream	5) Develop a clear vision to see your dreams

Table 3: Goals and Vision

Some of the prompt that can help you to create your vision:

1. **Personal growth**: What are my values? How can I develop my high priority values? How can I improve my awareness? What good habits I can develop to become best version of myself?
2. **Health (Physical +Mental +Emotional):** What is the current reality of my physical and mental health? How can I improve it? What are the tiny steps I can take? What are the triggers that are making me emotionally drain out? How can I heal them?
3. **Finance and career**: What is my current state of finance? How can I achieve my financial freedom? What is my long term goal in my career? Where I can see myself in the next five years?
4. **Relationship:** How can I improve my relationship with my family members and colleagues at my workplace?
5. **Impact (Contribution):** What gifts I can develop

and how can I add value to world by giving my life gift (talent) to them?

When we start asking the quality questions, we start connecting the dots. Seeing a vision at the beginning of the day or before going to sleep should be your ritual. As we know during that time we are in alpha state of our mind and our subconscious mind guide us to make it reality.

Advantage of having vision board:

1. It gives clarity to our life. We start painting how we want our life. We become more focused and our energy lasts longer.
2. Vision board is vehicle to reach our destination. It helps us to manifest the thing of our life.
3. It broadens our perspective towards life.
4. We feel inspired. It uplifts us.
5. We focus on what we want and what we don't want in life.

Goals:

"If you want to live a happy life, tie it to a goals, not to people or things"- ***Albert Einstein***

*"What you get by achieving your goals is not as important as what you become by achieving your goals"-**Zig Ziglar***

The most important things about setting goals is that it is not about achieving it. It is about the process that leads us to the goals. Have you ever set out a goal, achieved it and thought," now what?" It is true that you won't get lasting happiness even though you achieve it. That is what I am talking about. It is not about achieving the goals. It is about how the goal change our life. Striving for goals forces us to form new habits and that is priceless. When setting goals, the primary focus should be on direction rather than speed.

As we know there's an aviation concept 1-in-60 Rule. Here one-degree error in heading will cause a plane to miss its target by 1 mile for every 60 miles of fly.

The same concept applies to our goals. Any deviation can change the direction and it will be amplified by time and distance.

"The unexamined life is not worth living"-**Socrates**

When we change our perspective, automatically the speed towards achieving the goal changes.

The importance of delayed gratification is universally accepted. For example, consider the classic "marshmallow test" experiment: children's ability to delay eating of one marshmallow, so that they can get two marshmallows later is linked to a number of positive life outcomes, including academic success and healthy relationships and other goals. Being able to forgo immediate benefit to achieve bigger goals in future is viewed as a key skill.

As a project manager we implement various projects at site. Any project completion is end of goal for us. Initially thinking about the end goal and deadline was stressful for me even though system was there (like breaking the end goal with detailed schedule). The schedule is system which we have to follow. The same we have to follow with our personal goals. For example, if I want to lose 10 Kg by the end of 12 weeks, then instead of worrying about the end goal make a system /daily routine /habits to meet this target. Do not attach with the end goals by thinking about the process.

Following two factors are very important to achieve any goal:

1. Internal and
2. External factors.

The internal factor consists of you and your action. You have to back yourself for the goal set by you. The action is the sum of skillsets plus efforts to put into it plus time to achieve the goal.

The external factor consists of mentors, accountability partners, community, etc. that push you to achieve your goal.

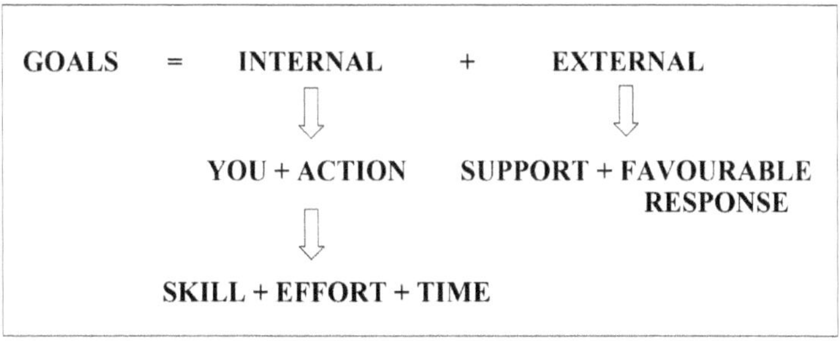

```
GOALS   =   INTERNAL          +   EXTERNAL
                ⇩                     ⇩
            YOU + ACTION      SUPPORT + FAVOURABLE
                ⇩                          RESPONSE
        SKILL + EFFORT + TIME
```

Figure 17: Factors to Achieve Any Goals

Favorable response is basically related to outcome. The people are required to get accomplish that outcome. That means you need people's support to manifest your goal. The bigger the goal, the bigger the commitment from your side.

Connect the goals with "why". Just imagine we set a goal and start working towards it for 5 days, 10 days, 30 days. But after that we forget it and dust cover it. Goals become guilty reminder for us and we self-talk like "we haven't kept aside time for it", "we don't know "why" of our goal even though we tried to find it", we don't know why we set the goals in first place.

There are many reasons why we failed to achieve our goals:

1. Not feeling like I deserve to succeed and feeling drained
2. Not being clear what we want in life
3. Trying to achieve too many new things in one go
4. Giving up when faced with obstacles
5. We get discouraged if it takes longer than we thought
6. We don't have a plan to achieve the goal

Most of us don't have strong reason to achieve the goal. Having a strong "why" will help you to say no to failure and find ways to keep going when things aren't straightforward or working in your favour."

I highly recommend this book for you "Start with Why by Simon Sinek". First, understand how scientifically we act when we crave for the "why". The limbic brain controls all of our emotions, behaviours, and decision making ability. It doesn't understand the language of the "gut decision". The neocortex brain controls all our logic, arguments, rational thought. The limbic brain is quite powerful and often contradicts or beat out our rational neocortex brain.

When we set a goal, neocortex has all the reasons why you should go to gym, develop a habit of getting at 5 AM in morning, or quit a smoking. But limbic brain wants us to feels good. Getting up early at 5 AM and stopping the smoking does not feel attractive or desirable to this brain.

You can trick the limbic brain if you add the feel good factors like giving voice to your "why". When we dig holes in sand at beach until we find the water like the same "why" is the shovel and "values" are water. We have to go deeper and dig our values. Once you find, attach the emotions in it and that's the way to trick it. As said earlier our limbic brain understand the language of emotions and that can be achieve by using above method.

Goals becomes easier when the purpose and why behind the goals is clear. We also eliminate all the distraction by doing it. Our goals must be congruent with our values and vice versa. Our values define what is important in life and defines our belief. We organize our entire life around these values and beliefs only.

Showing up:

When it comes to achieving goal, we start strong gathering momentum as we go. Then we get derailed or fall short of hopes. Take the example of new year resolution we make a promise to us, but we fail to sustain it. After that we start sabotaging us. Falling short of goals creates a negative cycle of discouragement that hinders our future action. Instead of moving forward we move backward.

"There is nothing more daring than showing up, putting ourselves out there and letting ourselves to be seen." -**Brene Brown**

In the beginning, showing up is even more important than being succeeding because if you don't build the habit of showing up, then you'll never have anything to improve in the future. Showing up look simple but practically it is not always easy. Sometime it is hardest things to do. It is the most vital step to living a life of what you are capable of just by "Showing up" and that brings up discipline, resilient, compassionate, and makes you more focused on your goals. Any inspiring positive change happens first by "showing up". When we commit to "showing up", you make promise to yourself. The self-commitment and accountability boost the self-esteem and self-worth. That means you value yourselves and your goal and prioritize them. Showing up is not just a physical act, but a choice to seize opportunity, confront challenges, enhance the relationship, grow personally and professionally, and build a network. It has profound importance being in present and making difference in your life and those around you. By showing up you become a part of solution, decision and cheerleader for someone else.

"80% of success is showing up."-**Woody Allen**

Your intention of showing up will result in great future.

Building Habits:

New Goals require changes in our daily routine. As we know our subconscious mind is the habit mind. It is like an ocean. By developing a routine, we fixed a habits. Habits are repetition and it is mother of all skill. Our subconscious mind understands the language of repetition. You require less efforts once it fit deep down into your subconscious mind. Let's enjoy the process of habits building and end result of goal will be taken care by the universe. For example, writing a book was major goal for me because no one in my family had written the book, so I decided to develop a habit of writing at least 10 lines every day. To increase my knowledge, I develop a habit of reading 10 pages a book every day. Gradually my writing and reading speed increased. Let's learn more about habit building process below.

1. **SMART Goals and Break it**: As we know goals should be SMART; Specific, Measurable, Achievable, Relevant, Time bound. Knowing end results of goal gives you the direction. But we have to bring visibility in our goal, and we can do it by breaking our goal in small manageable activity or chunks. Focusing on the small chunk bring us near to our goals every day.
2. **Changing the Belief System**: Our past failure of achieving the goals may trigger our subconscious mind with fear, anxiety, and doubts. We have to remove all our disempowering belief with right question and evidence so that it can be transformed to empowering belief system. The question we can ask: a) What's something that I know is holding me back? Identify

and write down your potential obstacles, excuses, fears, or barriers, and how you will navigate them, b) Which is an area I know very little about it and I am embarrassed for same (it will improve my life if will do it). c) You're on your death bed reflecting back on life? What mattered most in this reflection? What's the one thing that can bring you closer to this vision of a life that was well lived?

3. **Measure the Progress**: As the saying goes, "What gets measured, gets done". By reviewing the daily activities, we can reflect and state that we are on right path. Having an accountability partner with whom we can review our goals and can also share our pros and cons (or concern to them).

4. **Writing down the Goals**: A Harvard Business School has done study on goal setting. They asked the simple question in this study like "Have you set or written goals and created a plan to achieve them"? Following was the result of this study: a) 84% of entire class had not set goals. b) 13% of the class had set written goals but were no having any concrete plans. c) 3% of the class had both written and concrete plans to achieve their goals.

The school has monitored all these students up to 10 years. 10 years later when they measured they found that 13% of the class who had written goals were making 2 times more money than the 84% class who had no goals. 3% of class who had written and created concrete plan to achieve their goals were making 10 times more money than 97% of class.

Writing goals is always important. By writing we allow our body parts get active. By writing, we add thinking and feeling. As we know repetition is mother of all skill. Our subconscious mind understands the language of repetition. Once we be emotional for our goals (by adding feeling), we then automatically start to take the actions.

Mediation and Forgiveness:
Mediation:
"Meditation is painful in the beginning but it bestows immortal bliss and supreme joy in the end" -**Swami Sivananda.**

Mediation brings the stillness. As a human, we have to go through a lot of challenges on daily basis. We know our brain is supercomputer. Managing the 60 to 70 thousands thoughts per day along with emotions is really a challenge job for our mind.

Can you imagine what type of turbulence our mind can go through while dealing with the thinking. I personally feel mediation must be part of our daily life. Any machine need to work effectively and need preventive measure and maintenance to avoid any breakdown, the same is applied to human as we get overwhelmed by thoughts, emotions and we have to slow down it by using mediation as a tool (as a preventive measure to maintain our mental health).

During my college days I came to know the importance of mediation, but I was not aware about how to do it. I used to sit quietly and were simply focusing on breathing (inhale and exhale). It was little painful initially but after few days it became part of my daily rituals.

Every morning before I start my day and every night before I go to bed, I meditate as suggested by my mentor. It tunes my day. Mediation and visualizing the future self is great practice (when combine). The feeling I get after the practice is superb.

There is no bad mediation or good mediation. Only by practice we can feel the mediation.

Following are the important functions of different parts of our brain:

1. Grey matter which involved in muscle control and sensory perception, including emotions, memory, speech, seeing, hearing, and decision making
2. The Prefrontal cortex which is responsible for decision making
3. Amygdala which controls the emotional response
4. Hippocampus responsible for memory and learning

Practicing meditation helps you to control all the important parts of the brain and you also become aware of the workings of your subconscious mind. The more you meditate, the more likely you will be to tune into your deepest desires (or manifest your life goals fast). Mediation gives a lot of spiritual strength, peace, new vigour and vitality. It is the best mental tonic. You start to generate pure thoughts, blissful experiences, clear mental images once meditation becomes part of your life. The purpose of mediation is to slow down our brain waves from beta state to alpha state, the most relaxing state of our mind. This is the state where we find ourselves calm.

Consider the two cases here. The person A and B priming the day as per their choice they made. The Person A wake up in the morning and start checking the mobile, watches news, plays a video game whereas Person B wake up in the morning, just relax and practice the mediation and visualizes the day in advance. According to you who will feel great? Person A or B. Of course, the Person A will feel tired, anxious and will attract all the negative emotion and Person B will feel joyful and happy. Both Person A and B had conditioned their mind in different ways based on their choices.

Meditation serves as a gateway to access the realm of subconscious mind. It allows individuals to break free from deeply ingrained thought patterns and beliefs. By consistently engaging in meditation over the course of a week, individuals can create new neural pathways and can also overwrite old and limiting programs.

The Advantage of Meditation:

Practicing meditation consistently and correctly, can lead to lasting changes in our behaviour and outlook. They shape our daily lives. Following are the benefits of meditations.

1. **Cultivating Emotional Stability:**

Emotional stability is a valuable trait that we can strive

through emotional regulation and self-awareness. Through understanding our own emotions and how to manage them, we can become more emotionally balanced (or can manage our emotion like stress in better way), and can reduce our risk of mental and emotional breakout. We can learn how to recognize our triggers and how to manage them by using relaxation techniques and cognitive strategies such as reframing old belief and accepting the new one. The true sign of a meditator is that she has disciplined her mind by freeing it from negative emotions. Considering its neuroplasticity nature, our brain has the ability to rewire itself in response to repeated experience and can convert it into the quality ones.

2. **Enhancing Attention and Focus:**

   You can use strategies from the book Altered Traits by Daniel Goleman, which instructs readers on how to improve their focus and concentration levels. We can increase our attention span by engaging in physical activity and meditation, or taking deliberate breaks throughout the day. Specific strategies like concentrating on one task at a time can also be utilized. We can also break down tasks into smaller components, and utilize technology to help us stay on track.

3. **Cultivating Resilience:**

   Let's learn how to develop resilience here. To bounce back from adversity or setbacks and stay motivated, even when facing challenges, is what resilience is all about. Resilience can be developed by developing

self-compassion, being aware of your thoughts, seeking support from your community, and engaging in meaningful activities.
4. **Developing Self-Awareness:**

This part teaches us the importance of self-awareness. Self-awareness is the ability to understand our thoughts, feelings, and behaviours, and how they influence our environment and experiences. Self-awareness can be cultivated through journaling, mindfulness, and by engaging in meaningful conversations with others. By doing so, we can gain a better understanding of our strengths and weaknesses and use them to our advantage in order to reach our goals.

Forgiveness:

"Forgive others not because they deserve forgiveness, but because you deserve peace." – **Buddha**

Forgiving people is not always easy. There are 2 types of Forgiveness: Decisional and emotional forgiveness.

Decisional Forgiveness is easy. Here, we have conscious choice to replace ill will with good will. We think good about people who hurt us. We no longer wish for bad things to happen to other individuals.

Emotional forgiveness is little challenging and take times. Here we move away from negative feeling and no longer stuck in it. Experts says, this often happens when you think about the offender, or something triggers the memory. You still suffer from the adverse consequences of the action you done in the past and it erupts in the form of emotions. Feel it and consider it just an emotion. Forgive to the people and incidences.

Forgiveness gives us a lot of healing power for both our mind and body. Once we start Practicing forgiveness we feel calm and relax. As we know brain has the capacity to produce five type of waves.

Human brain waves were first recorded by Hans Berger in 1925 and by 1950 EEG detecting machines became very popular. Below table shows the human brain wave and its frequency.

Table 4: Human Brain Waves

GAMMA (31-100Hz)	Insight Peak Focus. Expanded consciousness
BETA (16-30 Hz)	Alertness, Concentration, Cognition
ALPHA (8-15 Hz)	Relaxation, Visualization, Creativity
THETA (4-7Hz)	Mediation, Intuition, memory
DELTA (0.1-3Hz)	Detached, Awareness, Healing, Sleep

These brainwaves are an indication of emotion and type of thinking. Higher frequency brainwaves are associated with higher levels of stress and alertness, while lower brainwaves are associated with intuition, relaxation, and creativity. The average person produces high frequency beta waves. Monk produces low frequency alpha waves. The alpha state is key to inspiration, genius-level intelligence, peak performance, balanced emotional capacity, increased immunity, and even total control of our mind. Through meditation, we can cultivate a deep sense of forgiveness, which trains our brains to operate on a completely different wavelength.

There are many benefits of forgiveness and a lot of study has done on it. The Forgiveness practice removes the toxicity from our mind and body. It heals us completely. Resentment and animosity carry mental, emotional, and physical pains that must be released by practicing forgiveness.

Forgiveness is about being honest with your emotions and changing your perception of yourself. Dr. Beckwith of Mind Valley explains that forgiveness moves you away from the victim consciousness (a state where the core traits are blaming others, making excuses, rationalizing, justifying your choices, and refusing to take responsibility).

What forgiveness allows you to do is that it truly place yourself in the driver's seat of your own life. It lets you guide your feelings and behaviors because you're now in charge of transforming and transcending these emotional states that brings you down.

Forgiveness is a crucial component in our spiritual growth. When we hold on to anger, resentment, and other negative emotions, we create blocks that prevent us from connecting with our higher selves and the world around us. In contrast, forgiveness helps us to cultivate a sense of empathy and compassion, and open our hearts to the beauty and love that surrounds us

The benefits of forgiveness are not just spiritual, but also physical and emotional. Research has shown that forgiveness can lead to reduced stress, improved immune function, and better overall health. By releasing negative emotions and focusing on forgiveness, we can create a positive feedback loop that nourishes our mind, body, and spirit.

The 5 Stages of Forgiveness:

Forgiveness is a process, not an immediate goal. Here are the five stages to get you move towards healing:

#1: Have the willingness to forgive. It can be a challenging task, but a fulfilling one. Identify what you need to forgive and why (or if) you're struggling to do so. If you are unwilling to forgive and hold on to your pain, you'll continue to be stuck in a place of suffering.

#2: Practice forgiveness through meditations, affirmations, journaling, or other means, offer your pain and hurt to the universe. Let it go.

#3: Be willing to see things from another person's perspective. Put yourself in the other person's shoes and try to understand why they behaved the way they did. Now, think back to a time when you were the offender. Doing this may help you to be compassionate and remember that everyone makes mistakes.

#4: Wish them well. Holding a grudge is detrimental to your well-being. So, wish them well and be on your way.

#5: Do something symbolically to send positive energy.

Whether you decide to reconcile or remove the person from your life, send them some good vibes. After all, as the Law of Attraction states, like attracts like. So, when you think good, you attract good.

Let's assess the questions below:

• When you think back to what happened, does it cause a trigger?

• How does the energy feel when you think of the person or event? Does it feel heavy? Or does it feel light?

• Do you feel like the love you have for yourself and your capacity to love has strengthened?

Commit to the process and you'll eventually find yourself feeling lighter and happier. All the above tools I practices on daily basis in the evening before going to bed. Love is higher energy which can be gain by forgiveness. When I had a bad day at office or I hurt anybody I try to follow the following steps to feel relax:

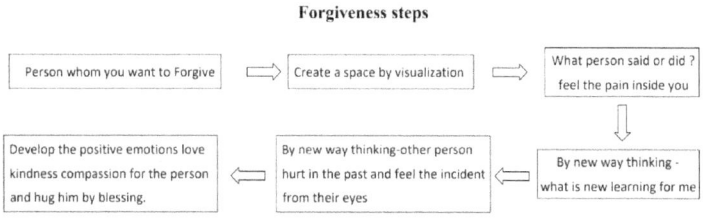

Figure 18: Steps involved in Forgiveness Practice

Feeling is main thing. Feel from Heart. Heart is more powerful than brain. Heart is center of our soul and oneself.

Feeling or emotions emits powerful magnetic field, the stronger the elevated emotions like love, kindness, compassion the stronger the magnetic field. Heart produces the strongest magnetic field in our body and that is 5000 times greater in strength compare to magnetic field produced by the brain. The impact is more when we start forgiving by using our heart as a medium.

Chaotic, anxious mind cannot forgive the person. So we have to calm the mind with relaxation technique. Meditation is one of the tools and I use it for forgiveness. Another tool is journaling, where one can express their feelings by writing and learn from the incident, then forgive the person/people who caused it.

By blessing something, we free our hurtful emotions, allowing us to heal more deeply, rather than keeping them buried and unresolved. To lubricate our emotions, we must acknowledge (bless) all aspects of those hurtful things: such as those who made us suffer, the cause of the suffering, and those who witness the outcome.

"Wherever there is a human being, there is an opportunity for a kindness."-**Seneca**

The following forgiveness affirmation tools can help you to remove the pain:

1. I live and let live
2. I forgive myself so that I can forgive others
3. The past is done. I now live in the present
4. I forgive so that I can have inner peace

Following are the advantage of Forgiveness:

1. **Forgiveness reduces stress**: Holding onto grudges and resentment can affect our mental and physical health. Forgiveness can help you reduce stress and anxiety, leading to better and overall well-being.
2. **Forgiveness improves relationships**: Forgiveness can help repair broken relationships and improve communication. It can also help you develop more profound, meaningful connections with the people in your life.
3. **Forgiveness promotes self-acceptance**: Forgiving others helps you accept yourself and your mistakes. It can also help you let go of self-blame and guilt.
4. **Forgiveness enhances emotional well-being**: Forgiveness can help you feel more positive emotions, such as peace and happiness, which can lead to greater emotional well-being.
5. **Forgiveness improves physical health**: Forgiveness has been linked to improved heart health, lower blood pressure, and a stronger immune system.
6. **Forgiveness can lead to personal growth**: Forgiveness can help you learn from your experiences and grow.
7. **Forgiveness helps you move on from the past**: Holding onto grudges can keep you stuck in the past, preventing you from moving forward. Forgiveness can help you let go of the past and focus on the present.

8. **Forgiveness can lead to greater empathy and compassion**: Forgiving others can help you develop greater empathy and compassion for others, leading to more fulfilling relationships.
9. **Forgiveness can help you find inner peace**: Forgiving others can help you find inner peace and a sense of calm, which can lead to greater overall well-being.
10. **Forgiveness can help you create a better future**: Forgiving others can help you create a better future for yourself and the people around you.

Forgiveness is not always easy, and it's not always possible. Forgiveness, however, provides many benefits. It can help you reduce stress, improve relationships, and enhance your overall well-being.

"The weak can never forgive. Forgiveness is the attribute of the strong" -**Mahatma Gandhi**

Visualization:

"Logic will get you from point A to point B. Imagination will take you everywhere else."-**Albert Einstein**

Visualization is the process of creating mental images or pictures in one's mind. It involves using sensory information and the imagination to simulate experiences and situations that feel real, despite not being physically present.

However, when we visualize a particular event or situation in advance, we essentially trick our brains into thinking that it is already familiar with the event or challenge that we are visualizing now, so it becomes less mistrustful.

We seize the opportunity by taking risk if it leads us towards our dreams (visualization).

Our intention defines our creative visualization. Following three elements that define our intention.

Intention = Desire +Belief +Acceptance

Intention is the starting point which brings clarity at first level. Through intention only we clear out our way and say to universe "This is what I want and I am ready to receive it. The intention is like the radar of a ship that tracks your voyage of manifestation.

Creative visualization is not just a technique, ultimately it is a state of consciousness. In visualization we use imagination to create a clear image, idea or feeling or something you wish to manifest. Then you continue to focus on idea, feeling or picture regularly by giving it a positive energy until it become objective reality, in other words, until you achieve what you have been imagining. Visualization can be a powerful tool for rewiring your brain and improving your ability to perform certain tasks or achieve certain outcome.

When we visualize the specific action or goal, same area of brain gets activated. Visualization is creating mental blueprint of our desire. Visualize it clearly, and feel that it is already happening. Close your eyes and imagine the life you want. The brain doesn't understand the difference between reality and imagination. It starts to wire itself to match your inner vision. The more you practice this, the more brain adapts to new reality. The feeling will be same like real one. As per neuroplasticity the brain gets rewired based on your thoughts and emotions, so if you consistently see and feel the life you desire, then it literally creates new neural connections or pathways and that support that reality. What sinks in brain is links in the brain. Coherence in brain leads to coherence in life.

Every day, you need to program yourself intentionally and do it till the time you realize your dream life. This is the most important thing you can do to create the life of your desire.

"If you're not being defined by a vision of the future, then all you'll be left with is memories from your past."- **Dr. Joe Dispenza**

In other words, if you aren't constantly visualizing and creating the new future that you desired in your mind, you're going to stay stuck in a loop with the same memories from your past (which will create the same experiences). We become what we think most of the time.

Michael Phelps one of the greatest swimmer who won the 28 medals in 4 Olympic game had said this "Visualization is one of the critical key to my achievement". The visualization skills that Phelps used each night helped him stay focused and confident under immense pressure. His coach Bob Bowman trained him in creative visualization from the age of 11.

Bowman had explained following steps of creative visualization of Michael Phelps:

1. **Start with relaxation techniques to prime yourself for visualization**: Close your eyes and just think

about what you want. Fooling your brain into believing that what you are mental rehearsing is real. Let the mind be calm and relax. In Visualization brain doesn't understand the difference in reality and imagined event. Each night Phelps would relax his body, limb by limb, from head to toes, before he would put on the video tape of his ideal performances. It becomes easier for you to create and watch your own movie, once you put yourself in a relaxed state.

2. **Use different perspectives when visualizing**: Michael used to have different perspective during visualization. For example, external visualization: where you are watching yourself performing from pool-side, or from a camera rolling across the pool deck like you are at home watching the race on TV. Internal Visualization: where you are viewing the race as you would be normally experiencing it, with goggles fogging up a little, the cold water splashing across your mouth, the lactic acid churning through your legs and arms. "Sometimes it's like you are in the stands watching yourself swim," says Bowman. "And sometimes it's like you are in the water, swimming."

3. **Prepare for all scenarios**: Mental imagery is a way to head off the anxiety and stress you experience when faced with the novelty of an uncertain situation. Phelps made a point to visualize things going well, things going poorly, and of course, the worst case scenario. By giving himself countless dress rehearsals ahead of time, he was calm and ready when it came to

getting down to business. "When I would visualize," Phelps says "It would be what you want it to be, what you don't want it to be, what it could be. You are always ready for whatever comes your way.

4. **Make your visualization as real as possible by engaging all your senses**: "The key to visualization is that it has to be very vivid," says Bowman. Michael used to Imagine the cold water on shaved skin. The lens of goggles sinking into face. The eerie quiet between take-your-marks and go. The more details sensations you fill in your visualizations, the more authentic the experience will be. Research has found that when we incorporate the little details that generate credibility, our brain is more willing to buy-in.

5. **Visualizing training is no different from any other training**: Visualization is effective when it is done consistently and repeatedly, to the point that when you get up on the block, your brain has the calm and poised sensation of having been there a ton of times. It has to be rehearsed many, many times," Bowman notes. "By the time Michael gets up on the blocks to swim in the World Championships or Olympics, he's swum that race hundreds of times in his mind before he gets up there.

Thus, it is clear from above that once we practice visualization our subconscious mind doesn't understand the difference between reality and imagination and it help us to manifest the things fast.

Affirmation and Belief Incantation:

"I am the greatest! I am awesome! I am fearless and powerful! Muhammad Ali affirmed these words over and over again and then he became them.

In the book Greatest: My Own Story, the author Muhammad Ali says, "It's the repetition of affirmations that leads us to that new belief. And once that belief becomes a deep conviction, things begins to happen." He believed without a doubt that he was the best fighter of all time, and he even pushed this belief upon his opponents. He kept repeating to himself in the mirror that he is the greatest of all time.

Advantage of Mirror Affirmation:

1. Rewire Neuropathways
2. Increase your magnetism
3. Fosters grateful attitude
4. Improve body image and awareness
5. Strengthen resilience
6. Increase emotional intelligence
7. Promotes positive lifestyle
8. Reduce stress

"When a thought of anger, jealousy, fear or worry creeps in just say the affirmation. The way to fight darkness is with light –the way to fight cold is with heat -the way to overcome evils is

with good. Affirm the good, and the bad will vanish" -**Frederick Elias Andrews**.

Through repetition of affirming statements, the brain can form new neural pathways, which create physical connections to these repeated thoughts. Setting up the right affirmation, brain start changing little by little. We make neuron in brain that fire together and by creating affirmation we build the mental association. It basically alters our brain by rewiring or by activating neuroplasticity. The affirmation with elevated emotions like joy, gratitude, peace, love makes us to change our negative bias brain to positive ones. Repeated affirmations provides an experience that shapes connections. Studies in neuroscience have shown that repeating affirmations triggers the brain's reward centers, releasing feel-good neurotransmitters such as dopamine. By affirming we change our identity or the person we want to be.

Framework Creating positive affirmation: Effective affirmation reshape our thought, belief and our reality.

1. **Positive statement**: This is the foundation of any affirmation. Always remember affirm what do you want, not what you don't want. By doing this we direct our subconscious mind to focus on positivity. Positive affirmations create a sense of possibility and optimism. INSTEAD OF SAYING I AM NOT AFRAID which emphasized fear, we can reframe it

as "I AM FEARLESS". This revised affirmation reinforces the desired behaviour and confidence.
2. **Present tense:** It is important to create desire as if it is already exist. This signals our subconscious mind that the affirmation is our current reality. By doing this we cultivate the strong belief in our abilities and likelihood of achieving our goals for example, we can say "I am attracting abundance and success into my life" instead of "I will attract abundance and success someday."
3. **Emotions and visualization**: Elevated emotions like joy, peace, gratitude amplify the impact. Emotions is like catalyst which gives energy to the affirm word. In visualization we create a mental picture of our new identity.
4. **Consistency and repetition:** Repeating affirmations on daily basis or multiple times in a day reinforces the new thought patterns and beliefs that we are trying to instill in us. Consistency is key in rewiring the subconscious mind that gradually replace the old, limiting beliefs with positive and empowering ones.
5. **Belief and alignment:** Be in alignment with the statement. If we don't genuinely believe in the affirmation or feel resistance towards it, then subconscious mind reject it. Try to create feeling of belief and experience that. It helps you to affirm the new faith. Remove time line, all the doubts, anxiety, hesitation and put all mental and emotional energy into affirmation and belief.

If still there is resistance, doubts or negative thoughts arises during affirmation, then start writing the affirmation. Writing affirmation is very potent technique because written word has more power over our mind. Our energy level reach sky high by reading and writing.

Move your Body:

"Take care of your body. It is only place you have to live"-
Jim Rohn

Body is like temple for us. For me the fitness can be summarized as: nutritious food plus good sleep plus physical exercise. Having the nutritious food (vitamins and minerals rich food) is always good for our body. As a vegetarian, I include fruits, vegetables, and dry fruits in my daily diet.

Fasting has many benefits for our body. Research has shown that fasting helps in improving our metabolism, lowers blood sugar level, remove toxins and damage cells from our body that in turn reduces the chances of chronic diseases.

During sleep our body perform repairing and maintenance activity. In the book "Why We Sleep" author Matthew Walker says that sleep deprivation shortens our lifespan. Quality 8 hours of sleep is essential for us in today's time. Sleep improves our mood, we feel calm and relax. It helps us to maintain our energy level. It reduces the risk of many diseases like heart, strokes, and obesity. Awakening generates alpha brain waves. This waves pattern is available to us from the wakefulness state to till the time we go to bed, then it is replaced by theta waves pattern as we sleep. Before sleeping try to keep away any gadget (keep it beyond your reach). Watching news, and browsing social media is strictly prohibited before you sleep (as it impacts our body and mind). A good night's sleep can be achieved by meditating or reading a book before we go to bed.

Physical exercise is main ingredient to keep our body in shape. Even a simple exercise like walking, jogging, or yogasanas is good for our health. Bring the movement in body. Imagine when we feel stuck or overwhelmed, and if we move our bodies by jumping jacks or squatting, we feel energy throughout our bodies. By doing this, we release the happy chemical like DOSE (Dopamine, oxytocin, Serotonin and Endorphins). Also, when we are in happy state we can create anything and enjoy life to the fullest.

Universe design our destiny based on our Karma. Our words, actions and thoughts decides our faith and it gets transcribe into our Karma. Let's learn about it in the next chapter.

9

How Law of Karma Helps you to Live a Better Life

****

"Every moment of your life, you perform action – physically, mentally, emotionally, and energy-wise. Each action creates a certain memory. That is karma". – **Sadguru**

Karma literally means action or deed in Sanskrit. Karma is law of cause and effect or action and reaction. Its reminds us that our actions bear consequences. When we treat others with kindness and respect, then universe tends to respond in same way. When we sow negativity, it often finds its way back to us. Universe maintain its harmony, balance and equilibrium. Karma is always an invitation to practice compassion, kindness, and empathy.

Karma is the sum-total of works: good, bad and mixed- which an individual performs during his lifetime. It is the collective totality of man's actions. It is these actions that determine his future existence.

Accumulation of karma is determined only by your intention and the way you respond to what is happening to you. Over time, it is possible to become ensnared by your own unconscious patterns of behaviour.

*"Service is the rent we pay for a room on earth"-**Muhammad Ali***

Be good. Do good. No matter what. We rise by lifting others. Amidst life's complexities, its crucial to focus karma. By nurturing positive intentions and actions, we create a ripple effect of goodness. So seed of kindness, for what we send out into world, returns to shape our reality in same way. A simple gesture can have a profound impact on others. A genuine compliment, a kind word, a warm smile can brighten someone's day and make them feel valued and appreciated. Kindness doesn't usually cost anything.

"What goes around, comes around". We cannot blame anyone for the problems and trouble that we are facing. We are responsible for our own deeds, words, feelings and thoughts.

We cannot expect mango fruit by having a seed of apple. It is the universal truth that what a man sows, is what he will reap. If we want to create happiness, joy, abundance, prosperity in our lives, we must learn to sow the seeds of happiness, joy, abundance, prosperity. Therefore, karma implies the action of conscious choice-making.

If you are able to know and understand Karma properly, then you would be able to change and modify your destiny accordingly. Therefore, to get a specific result, you need to create actions that would inevitably lead you to that expectations or experiences.

My understanding on this subject got more intense by understanding the *Pranic* healing. Grand Master Choa Kok Sui had said this golden rule about the karma: Do unto others what you would have them do unto you", also, "Do not do unto others what you would not have them to unto you." This Golden Rule is actually the spiritual technique to create your future and destiny. It can be applied both positively (the yang form) and negatively (the yin form).

The Law of Karma, when applied positively, manifests as the Yang Golden Rule – "Do unto others what you would have do unto you". This rule can be applied to get what you want or desire. In other words, if you want to be helped in times of need, help others in need. If you want to be treated nicely, treat others nicely too. If you want your life to be blessed with prosperity and abundance, be charitable by helping people in need. If you want cordiality and harmony, then be cordial and courteous to others.

The Law of Karma can also be used to avoid undesirable things or events when applied as the Yin Golden Rule – "Do not unto others what you would not have them do unto you." Hence, if you do not want to be cheated or swindled, then treat others honestly and fairly. If you do not want to get hurt, refrain from hurting others. If you do not want to be judged, do not judge. If you do not want to experience hunger, feed the poor. If you do not want your goods to be stolen, do not take what does not belong to you.

These golden rules can be applied everywhere. If we want money and prosperity, first we have to donate money to poor people. If we do not want to be hungry or starve in our life, then we need to feed the people who do not have food for themselves. We need to help people in time of disasters and calamities so that we get help from others in the time of our needs. Practice giving in order to receive. This is how you will plant the seed of good karma for the future and as per the golden rule, this will be returned to you manifold in the future. Use the concept of Law of Karma to better your life.

Remember this three golden rule of Law of Karma:

1. Generate good karma
2. Avoid generating bad karma
3. Neutralize past negative karma.

We can neutralize the negative karma "learning the lesson that is to be learnt", and utilizing the "Law of Mercy" and "Law of Forgiveness". The Law of Mercy means that in order to receive mercy, one must always be merciful towards others. All forms of negative thoughts and emotions, injurious words and cruelty towards others must always be avoided. The Law of Forgiveness means that we should forgive and bless all those who have hurt us. It is necessary to forgive because it helps us to release all the pent-up negative emotions.

These laws are universal and they work on everything. Even our earth has Karma, our solar system has Karma. Initially, I was not ready to accept this law. I began to feel changes in myself as soon as I started practicing them. As per the law of gravity of Isaac Newton, if a person jumps off from the top of a building, then he/she will always go down and will never go up. The same way the law of Karma works. Every action has a reaction. It balances the energy. We should never doubt it.

During a coaching session, one of our group members was asking to our coach that "Why is her income not increasing? Our coach asked her this question in return "How much money she is donating to the needy? She answered that she is not doing any donations at all. Our coach then asked her to donate 10% of her earnings. Once she starts donating, she will see results after 2-3 months. If you want to increase your income, then donate the money. It's not about the money but imagine the blessings she must be getting from the person she is supporting through this act. Every act has a reaction in the form of energy. She will harness the energy of blessings here. Also, she will feel peace from the inside. It sometimes takes time, but law of karma works.

I like the idea of minimalism. When we own too many things, our lives get cluttered. But if you really think about it, we actually own nothing in life. Helping others or service to others gives direction to meaningful life. Our material attachment diminishes, when we start reaching for our higher self. We become more grateful for our life and people.

By conscious choice and action, we can overcome on our negative karma. If you like it or not, everything that is happening at this moment in your life is a result of the choices you've made in the past. Based on our belief and environment we make a choice. Based on choice we take an action. Quality action can be implemented by using following steps:

1. **Making conscious choice**: The choice we make influence our karma in two ways. Quality choices lowers the intensity or magnitude of situation (returning of karma). The second way choices also determine the quality of new karma being created and stored and released as future events in life, so we have to be conscious while making choice and keep asking these questions "Do these choices serve me? Are my decisions coming from my heart and higher self or my ego?
2. **Forgive**: This is important considering our spiritual growth. First accept the situation and do not carry the baggage of the emotions without judgement and evaluation and understand why it happened. Try to forgive whoever hurt you. From the Vedantic perspective, every hurt you encounter is the return of some Karma. If the postman fills your mailbox with

bills, don't spend the whole day hating the postman. Forgive and move on.

3. **Attitude of gratitude**: Try to be grateful for things in life and appreciate it. By doing this you release the negative Karma.
4. **Discover the Dharma**: Dharma is usually defined as purpose or truth. When you find your true purpose in life and live in total alignment with that, your actions will become spontaneously correct and you will create a good karma.
5. **Meditate**: Meditating regularly allows you to live from a high level of infinite possibilities instead of the limited ones you created from your past Karma. Meditation realigns you with your true self and leads you back to your true purpose (Dharma) and allows you to "wash" away bad Karma on all levels.
6. **Develop the abundance mindset**: During challenging times instead of seeing the problem see the opportunities by asking how can I learn and grow from this. If you see it as a problem, you can get drawn into lower energy, which recreates the same Karmic energy, and you make no progress. Looking for growth opportunities allows you to release the Karma and remain free to move ahead on your spiritual journey.

10

Conclusions

****

"I'd rather live in regret of failure than in never trying". –
M J Demarco

Everyone in the life evolves and has to go through various levels of life or we can summarize the life's journey of the person in the following ways:

Journey of Life 1: I walked down on new street and choose the side way to walk safely but there is huge pothole on the sidewalk and I fell into it. I am helpless and shouting for help. It's not my fault. Destiny takes a long time to get me out from here.

Journey of Life 2: I walked down on the same street again. There is huge pothole on the sidewalk. This time I pretended of not seeing it. I fell into it again. It's my fault now. Again destiny takes a long time to get me out of here.

Journey of Life 3: I walked down on the same street again. There is huge pothole on the same sidewalk. Second time I pretended of not seeing it. Now falling into it has become a habit for me. I am helpless, crying, shouting, frustrated. It's my fault and I have wired my brain for such a pity life. Then something inside said this to me "I could see it". I would have avoided the fall. My eyes are open. I know where I am. It's really my fault. Now, I have to get out of it immediately. I can't live a miserable life like this.

Journey of Life 4: I walked down on the same street. There is huge pothole on my sidewalk. I walked around it and look into it said this "This time I am lucky that I can avoid you". I have become conscious for my life now. Pretending falling into it for mercy was my mistake. Now let's walk down the main road.

Journey of Life 5: I walked down on the another street, there are many potholes on it. But I have become fearless for them and I can avoid them tactically. I become more wise.

I can relate the above story with me. I pretended not to see even though I fell into the pothole again and again. After certain period of time, I was comfortable to be inside it. After attending various workshop and seminars, I realized that these potholes are barrier on my main road to success. I read a lot of books and figure out various potholes of my life. I started to look solution for this problems and joined all the points and that came out in the form of 8 habits that I have mentioned in this book.

All the chapters discussed in this book are my life's learning. From being a shy person to writing this book and sharing it with the world is itself a great transformation for me. It's a learning that anyone can apply in their life and can bring the same changes. May the insight of this book help you to cultivate abundance mindsets and brings prosperity in your life.

11

Prosperity Gift for You

I have given goal writing format, gratitude journal, affirmations and habit tracker template at the end of this book for your use. This will help you build your habits in a better and faster way.

Goal Writing Format:

I am so happy and grateful that my goal of having -------- has manifested easily, joyfully, consistently by the great blessing of god and universe, so be it, so be it, so be it, thank you, thank you, thank you!

(-----specific goal with date to be put for example **my bestselling book by 15 -March-2024). Let's relook it below.**

I am so happy and grateful that my goal of having **my bestselling book by 15 -March-2024** has manifested easily, joyfully, consistently by the great blessing of god and universe, so be it, so be it, so be it, thank you, thank you, thank you!

Goal writing can be around seven spokes of life (spiritual, physical, intellectual, career, financial, family, and social).

Goal writing to be written before going to bed at night. Weekly review of the Goal to be done.

Gratitude Journal:

1. Before you start your day list down 10 things you are grateful for:

2. List 3 obstacles and what you learned from them.

3. List 3 things that make you feel good about the things you support and appreciate in others.

4. List 5 people who made your life little happier.

Affirmation to Practice:

1. Everyday in everyway, I am getting better, better, and better- ***Emile Coue***
2. I am fearless, powerful, active, energetic, healthy and wealthy
3. I am now attuned to my higher purpose in my life
4. I feel happy just being alive
5. Abundance is my natural state of being
6. My intention, thought, emotions create my life and destiny
7. The more I have, the more I have to give.

8. I am now attracting loving satisfying relationship into my life
9. I am totally independent of good or bad of others opinion.
10. I am grateful for what I have
11. I am consistent action taker

Habit Tracker Template:

Habits	Mon	Tue	Wed	Thu	Fri	Sat	Sun
Prayer	√	√	√	√	√	√	√

www.ingramcontent.com/pod-product-compliance
Lightning Source LLC
LaVergne TN
LVHW020442070526
838199LV00063B/4823